Target Marketing

Researching, Reaching and Retaining Your Target Market

THIRD EDITION

Linda Pinson

and

Jerry Jinnett

UPSTART
PUBLISHING COMPANY
Specializing in Small Business Publishing
a division of Dearborn Publishing Group, Inc.
Chicago, Illinois

Other books and software by the same authors:

Anatomy of a Business Plan
Keeping the Books
The Home-Based Entrepreneur
Steps to Small Business Start-Up
Automate Your Business Plan software

This publication is designed to provide accurate and authoritative information in regard to the subject matter covered. It is sold with the understanding that the publisher is not engaged in rendering legal, accounting, or other professional service. If legal advice or other expert assistance is required, the services of a competent professional person should be sought.

Publisher and Acquisitions Editor: Jere L. Calmes
Editorial Assistant: Becky Rasmussen
Production Manager: Karen Billipp
Cover Design: Jill Shimabukuro

© 1988, 1989, 1993, and 1996 by Linda Pinson and Jerry Jinnett

Published by Upstart Publishing Company,
a division of Dearborn Publishing Group, Inc.

Printed in the United States of America
96 97 98 10 9 8 7 6 5 4 3 2 1

Library of Congress Cataloging-in-Publication Data
Pinson, Linda.
    Target marketing : researching, reaching, and retaining your target market / Linda Pinson and Jerry Jinnett. --3rd. ed.
        p.   cm.
    Rev. ed. of: Target marketing for the small business / Linda Pinson and Jerry Jinnett. 2nd. ed. 1993.
    Includes index.
    ISBN: 1-57410-027-0 ✓
    1. Target marketing. 2. Small business--Management. I. Jinnett, Jerry. II. Pinson, Linda. Target marketing for the small business. III. Title.
HF5415.127.P56 1996   96-3411
658.8--dc20   CIP

Table of Contents

Introduction

The development of a good marketing plan is essential to your business success. Your product or service may be in demand and be competitively priced. You may have found the lowest prices for your supplies and may have secured adequate financing for your business. All of these items will be of no value if you have not taken the time to identify your customers through market research, found the means for your product or service to reach that market, and, once established, determined methods for retaining that customer base. The key word here is **time**. It takes time to research and develop a marketing plan, but it is time well spent.

There are professional firms and individual consultants who can conduct market research for you. These services conduct market surveys, compile data and make recommendations. Professional marketing studies may be too costly for the small or home-based business. Don't overlook non-professional sources for help with market research. Contact the business departments of the colleges and universities in your area. Often students majoring in Marketing are required to do marketing surveys and to prepare marketing plans as part of their course work. There generally is a nominal fee for this service. In return, you will be getting a marketing plan prepared by bright, motivated and energetic students who will be evaluated on the project.

Every state has a unique network of Small Business Development Centers that provide management and technical assistance to small businesses. Funding for these centers comes through the Small Business

Administration and from grants. Often these centers are operated through affiliation with a local community college or university. More than 700 of these centers across the nation offer free consulting services on financial planning and all other technical aspects of starting and running a small business.

Another resource is SCORE (Service Corp of Retired Executives), which has been administered by the U.S. Small Business Administration (SBA) since 1964. The purpose of both SCORE and the SBA is to help the entrepreneur get into business and stay there. SCORE offers seminars, workshops and free one-on-one counseling. If help is needed with marketing, a counselor with expertise in that area will be assigned.

You may choose to do your own market research and develop your own marketing plan. Most of the information you will need can be found in your public or college library and in the publications of the Department of Commerce, the Small Business Administration, and the Census Bureau. Additional information is available from trade associations and their publications and through the chambers of commerce. By doing your own market research and developing your own plan, you will have demystified marketing. You will learn all there is to know about your type of business.

Marketing has been defined as all of the activities involved in moving goods and services from the seller to the buyer. Marketing is **everything** you do to promote your business. The design of your business card and promotional materials, the way in which you present yourself, the attitudes of your employees, and the quality of your product or service all project the image or identity of your business. A person concerned with marketing must be consumer-oriented. A successful business owner views a product or service in an objective manner. Determine the identity of your business and carry it through in your product design, advertising and promotional materials.

This book has been designed to take the mystery out of marketing. It presents a step-by-step format for developing your marketing plan. The process has been divided into three parts:

The first section gives instruction in **researching the market**. You want to survey the market to determine current buying trends and to identify new products and services. You will learn how to construct, distribute and evaluate questionnaires as a means of testing the marketplace. The importance of evaluating the competition is stressed and the means for identifying your target market are shown.

Once your customer base has been identified, you will learn how to develop a strategy for **reaching that market**. In the second section of this book, we will examine what are known as the "five Ps" of marketing. You will position your product or service and enter the marketplace. Methods of distribution, location, pricing structure, timing of market entry, promotion and packaging all play a vital role in a successful marketing plan. Publicity and advertising methods are critical to reaching your customers. Advances in communications technology and an increasingly "wired" population have allowed customers to use computer online services, cable TV, and the information superhighway for information on new products and services.

Reaching your customers is not enough. The third section shows ways of **retaining your market**. One way of accomplishing this is by providing good customer service and achieving customer satisfaction. Customer complaints can be employee, location, product or service-oriented. You will be shown ways of anticipating and preventing these types of complaints. You will see how guarantees and warranties are the most powerful marketing statements a company can make. The importance of community involvement is stressed. You will learn how to communicate knowledge of your industry, how to find out what your customers have to say and how to maintain an open working relationship with staff and suppliers. It has been said that the best form of advertising is "word of mouth." A successful business is based upon customer and community loyalty.

Topic-specific resources and worksheets are located at the end of each chapter and more blank worksheets are located at the end of the book. The final sections of the book contain additional resource listings and a glossary. View the process of market research and planning as detective work. You are on the trail of the elusive "target market" and you won't get paid until you find it! The more "clues" or information you have, the more successful you will be in researching, reaching and retaining that customer and in having the satisfaction of selling your product or service.

PART I

Researching Your Target Market

✔ How to Survey the Market

✔ Protecting Your Idea

✔ The Use of Questionnaires

✔ Testing the Market

✔ Evaluating the Competition

✔ Finding Your Target Market

How to Survey the Market

In order to be successful, a business must know its market. Market research is an organized and objective way of learning about your customers. It involves finding out what a customer wants and needs and determining how your company can meet those wants and needs.

Market research: The systematic design, collection, analysis and reporting of data regarding a specific marketing situation.

Evaluate Current Buying Trends

One method of learning about customers, products and services is to look at what is being purchased and who is doing the purchasing. In marketing, this is known as evaluating trends. A **trend** is a behavior or buying pattern that lasts between five and ten years and is generally widespread. Current trends seem to be environmentalism, fantasy, relationships, unusual and "natural" spices and foods, family togetherness, and concern for health and aging.

Foods, cosmetics, and packaging materials are removing color additives and promoting themselves as "clear" or "crystal" as a response to health and environmental issues. The use of recycled paper has increased. Television programming is dominated by science fiction series, "relationship" sit-coms, and cooking shows. We see the trend toward family closeness and nostalgia shaping what consumers purchase. Popcorn sales and video rentals increase on the weekends and indicate the trend toward family evenings at home. The introduction of bread baking machines and the success of shops selling coffee beans indicate the appeal of a return to earlier "do-it-yourself" times. Advertising stresses "making our lives easier," features "senior citizens," and touts "environmental safety." Evidence of current trends surrounds us.

Fads seem to occur among smaller groups and last for only a year or two. Although large sums of money can often be made by being the first to present a fad, business longevity is tied to trends. The smart business person looks at the current trends, as well as those being predicted for the future, and finds ways of tailoring products or services to meet the needs of consumers in terms of those trends.

Don't underestimate personal observation as a means of tracking trends. A great deal can be learned about the buying habits in your area by watching the purchases made in the supermarket check-out line and the stores in the mall. What specialty shops are opening? What colors seem to be popular? What books are on the bestseller lists and what subjects do they cover? What foods are being featured in restaurants? When are most purchases made? Who is making these purchases?

Advertising: The practice of bringing to the public's notice the good qualities of something in order to induce the public to buy or invest in it.

Trends can be anticipated by analyzing television. On the "Cosby Show," Bill Cosby began wearing multicolored, patterned sweaters. A trend was started and we saw these fashionable sweaters in stores, in catalogs and in advertising. A variety of products provided a backdrop for Jerry Seinfeld's kitchen scenes; an increase in the sale of these products could be traced to their visibility on that television program. Beauticians received requests to duplicate Jennifer Aniston's hair style following the popularity of the show, "Friends." Television has a great influence on our lives. Watch program's with a marker's eye. What current shows are popular, what segment of the population do they appeal to, and what new products or services are being showcased?

Reading the trade journals and publications for your field can also give you that "edge." In 1986, the **Gift Reporter**, a trade journal for gift retailers, indicated that there was an interest in products featuring dinosaurs. We now see dinosaurs as stuffed animals, as pasta shapes, on calendars, coffee mugs, and T-shirts, and as stars of cartoons and feature-length movies! While many may have thought this would turn out to be a fad, a decade of exposure has proven interest in dinosaurs to be a trend. Observations at a recent California Gift Show indicate an interest in butterflies, seahorses, fish and roosters. Will these become part of the new trends?

New Products

A careful examination of trends can often point the way to a new product. You may wish to develop a newsletter covering health, family or environmental issues. The desire for family closeness has brought back an interest in card and board games. According to the Toy Manufacturers of America, sales for adult board games topped $120 million in 1991, which is an increase of $10 million over the previous year. Perhaps you can develop a new game. If you have a restaurant, you may meet the new market interest in nostalgia, convenience and health by creating take out "home-cooked" meals.

Inventor Shows enable inventors and manufacturers to get together to put new products on the market. The chamber of commerce, the Small Business Administration and local convention centers will have listings of inventor shows in your area. The U.S. Department of Commerce has listings of foreign manufacturers that are seeking U.S. companies to manufacture and sell certain products to the U.S. market. This resource will be listed in the government section of your phone directory.

Chamber of commerce: An organization of business people designed to advance the interests of its members. There are three levels: national, state and local.

New Services

Just as analysis of trends can indicate a market for new products, a need for new services will also be evident. With the popularity of the Cabbage Patch Doll®, many dry cleaning establishments anticipated the need for cleaning these "well-loved" dolls and provided this service. Many desktop publishing and word processing services are being operated as home-based businesses. This equipment will need service and repair. Perhaps you could develop a mobile repair business for computer equipment. Again, trade associations and their publications can alert you to new services. Look for new products and equipment that will need future service and repair.

Need: A state of perceived deprivation.

Summary

A new company will examine trends, find new products and identify new services in terms of developing a business that will fill a consumer need. It has been said that to compete in today's economy, a business must be able to generate income from nine different sources! It is important to first focus on the product or service that you are most capable of delivering. Your market research will identify other needs of your target market, which you can offer when appropriate and financially feasible. Existing businesses will look for areas in which they can expand. For example, bookstores are expanding their product lines to include magazines, audio and video tapes, CDs and records. They are hosting "mystery reading clubs" and children's reading hours to generate interest and increased sales. They are subletting meeting and conference space. Many are also including expresso bars and coffee shops. Service businesses are offering

Service business: A business that performs a task or service for the customer rather than supplying a tangible product.

complementary product lines that enhance their services. Photographers are offering picture framing, teaching classes, and writing "how-to" articles for magazines and newspapers. An individual offering delivered "home-cooked" meals could write a column for the food section of the local newspaper and could develop a cookbook. Remember that marketing is dynamic: your customers' likes and dislikes are constantly shifting. Be alert for the changing market and plan what you can do to compete.

Resources

Books

Anderson, Rolf, *Atlas of the American Economy: An Illustrated Guide to Industries and Trends*, (Washington, DC: Congressional Quarterly Books, 1995).

Husch, Tony, and Linda Foust, *That's a Great Idea* (Berkeley, CA: Ten Speed Press, 1987).

Popcorn, Faith, *The Popcorn Report* (New York: HarperCollins, 1992).

Zandel, Irma, and Richard Leonard, *Targeting the Trend Setting Consumer* (Homewood, IL: Business One Irwin, 1992).

References

Encyclopedia of Associations. Reference book published by Gale Research, Detroit, MI.

National Trade and Professional Associations of the U.S. Reference book published by Columbia Books, Washington, DC.

Agencies

American Marketing Association
250 S. Wacker Drive, Suite 200
Chicago, IL 60606
(312) 648-0536

Offers research and seminars to marketers, sales managers, market researchers and others.

U.S. Department of Commerce
Contact the local field office listed in the phone directory and request information for the *International Commerce Magazine.* Its "Licensing

Opportunities Section" lists foreign products available for licensing for sale and/or manufacture in the United States.

Office of Inventions and Innovations
National Bureau of Standards
Washington, DC 20234

Request a listing of the major inventor shows throughout the United States.

U.S. Small Business Administration
P.O. Box 46521
Denver, CO 80201
(800) 827-5722 (SBA Small Business Answer Desk)

Use the rotary phone option, speak to a representative and request a *Directory of Publications*. Or contact your area or district SBA or SCORE office.

Ideas Into Dollars: This publication identifies the main challenges in product development and provides a list of resources to help inventors and innovators take their ideas into the marketplace. PI 1...$2.00

Protecting Your Idea

When you are developing your product or service, you want to make certain that you are not infringing on the rights of others. You also want to get protection for your own work. Don't let the fear of having your idea stolen keep you from the marketplace. In order to develop and sell ideas, you have to disclose them. The development and market research stage is a good time to review the safeguards of a disclosure letter and a journal, as well as protection under the federal law of copyright, trademark and patent.

Disclosure Letter

One way of protecting your idea is through the use of a disclosure letter. This is a letter outlining your idea for your new product or service, detailing the research and work you have done to date and citing the people you have contacted while doing your research. Date the letter and have it notarized. The purpose of the disclosure letter is to verify the date on which the idea was yours. Place the letter in a sealed envelope and file it in a safe place.

Journal

Establishing a date by means of a disclosure letter is not enough. You must be able to demonstrate that you are involved in an **active business** as opposed to a **passive business** activity. An active business is able to show continuous work and progress in developing the idea into a viable product or service. This may be done by keeping a **log** or **journal**. This is a diary that will show daily entries verifying ongoing work.

To be considered a legal document, the log must be a bound book (not loose-leaf), have consecutively numbered pages, be written in ink and contain no erasures. If you make an error, line through it, initial it and make the correction. Do not use correction fluid. Include information regarding the people to whom you have spoken about your idea and the dates and locations of the meetings. The journal and the disclosure letter give you the security you need to begin your market research. A sample journal page (p. 18) with entries has been included at the end of this chapter.

Copyright

Copyright is a legal protection provided to the authors of "original works of authorship that are fixed in a tangible form of expression." The fixation does not need to be directly perceptible, so long as it may be communicated with the aid of a machine or device. Copyrightable works include the following categories:

1. Literary works.

2. Musical works, including any accompanying words.

3. Dramatic works, including any accompanying music.

4. Pantomimes and choreographic works.

5. Pictorial, graphic, and sculptural works.

6. Motion pictures and other audiovisual works.

7. Sound recordings.

8. Architectural works.

9. Electronic media.

These categories cover a broad area. For example, computer programs are registered as "literary works," and maps and architectural plans are registered as "pictorial, graphic, and sculptural works."

On March 1, 1989, the law for copyright protection was changed. Under the present law, copyright protection is secured automatically when the work is created, and a work is "created" when it is fixed in a copy or phonorecord for the first time. "Copies" are material objects from which a work can be read or visually perceived, either directly or with the aid of a machine or device, such as books, manuscripts, sheet music, film, videotape or microfilm. "Phonorecords" are material objects that embody fixations of sounds, such as audio tapes and phonograph disks.

For works first published on or after March 1, 1989, the use of the copyright notice is optional although highly recommended. Before March 1, 1989, the use of the notice was required on all published works, and any work first published before that date must bear a notice or risk loss of copyright protection.

Use of the notice is recommended because it informs the public that the work is protected by copyright, identifies the copyright owner, and shows the year of the first publication. The notice for visually perceptible copies should contain the following three elements:

1. **The symbol** © (the letter c in a circle), or the word "Copyright," or the abbreviation "Copr."

2. **The year of first publication** of the work.

3. **The name of the owner of copyright** in the work or an abbreviation by which the name can be recognized, or a generally known alternative designation of the owner.

Example: © 1996 Jane Doe

The "C in a circle" notice is used only on "visually perceptible copies." Certain types of works such as musical, dramatic and literary works may be fixed by means of sound in an audio recording.

Generally, no publication or registration in the Copyright Office is required to secure a copyright. There are, however, certain advantages to registration:

1. Registration establishes a public record of the copyright claim.

2. Before an infringement suit may be filed in court, registration is necessary for works of U.S. origin and for foreign works not originating in a Berne Union Country. (For clarification, request Circular 93 from the Copyright Office).

3. If made before or within five years of publication, registration

will establish prima facie evidence in court of the validity of the copyright and of the facts stated in the certificate.

4. If registration is made within three months after publication of the work or prior to an infringement of the work, statutory damages and attorney's fees will be available to the copyright owner in court actions.

5. Copyright registration allows the owner of the copyright to record the registration with the U.S. Customs Service for protection against the importation of infringing copies.

Registration may be made at any time within the life of the copyright. To register a work, send the following three elements in the same envelope or package to the Copyright Office (the address is listed in "Resources" at the end of this chapter):

1. A properly completed application form. (Free application forms are supplied by the Copyright Office.)

2. A nonrefundable filing fee of $20.00. (Copyright fees are adjusted at five year intervals, based on increases in the Consumer Price Index. The next adjustment is due in 1997. Contact the Copyright Office in January of 1997 for the new fee schedule.)

3. A nonreturnable deposit of the work being registered. The deposit requirements vary in particular situations and special deposit requirements exist for many types of work. If you are unsure of the deposit requirement for your work, write or call the Copyright Office and describe the work you wish to register.

A copyright registration is effective on the date the Copyright Office receives all of the required elements in the acceptable form, regardless of how long it then takes to process the application and to mail the certificate of registration. The copyright protection is for the lifetime of the author plus an additional 50 years after the author's death. The use of the copyright notice is the responsibility of the copyright owner and does not require advance permission or registration with the Copyright Office. The address and phone numbers for the Copyright Office are listed at the end of this chapter.

Trademark

A **trademark** is a word, symbol, unique name, design, logo, slogan or some combination of these used by a company to identify its products. A **service mark** identifies and distinguishes a service rather than a product. A **trade name** is used to designate a company rather than a product or service. In general, the federal trademark statute covers trademarks, service marks, and words, names or symbols that identify or are capable of distinguishing goods or services. Copyright registration cannot be made for names, titles or other short phrases or expressions.

Until recently, trademark and service mark rights were granted based on use. An application to register a trademark in the U.S. could only be made if the mark had actually been used for a product or service that had been offered for sale through interstate commerce. Recent changes in the U.S. trademark law now allow a company or individual to file a trademark application for the purpose of "reserving" that trademark for future licensing and to protect the trademark for up to three years before it is actually used in commerce. These are known as "intent-to-use" applications.

Trademark renewals take place every 10 years. There is a fee for renewal and a penalty for late renewal applications.

Although there is no requirement to file, registration provides certain legal protection to trademark owners in the United States. Application and filing forms are available from the Patent and Trademark Office, which is listed at the end of this chapter. Registration requires three steps:

1. A properly completed registration form.

2. A nonrefundable filing fee of $245.00 (effective 12/3/93).

3. Physical representation of the mark.

There is a standard format for the use of the trademark symbol. The letters "TM" must be placed after every use of the trademark or symbol, like this: ™. The letters "SM" are used for a service mark. Once the trademark registration has been completed and confirmed, the symbol R with a circle around it, ®, will be placed after every use of the trademarked word or symbol.

These marks serve to identify and distinguish an owner's products, goods or services from those of the competition. They can serve as good marketing tools, provided the quality and reputation of goods and services is maintained.

Patent

When you have an idea for a new invention or process, it is important to analyze that idea for originality and patentability. One of the most difficult and crucial steps to securing a patent is to determine "novelty." Establishing novelty involves two things:

1. Analysis according to specific standards set down by the Patent Office.

2. Determining if anyone has patented it first.

The only sure way to do this is to conduct a search of Patent Office files. To help make these files available to the public, the federal government established the Depository Library Program. These libraries offer the publications of the U.S. Patent Classification System, contain current issues of U.S. Patents, maintain collections of earlier issued patents and provide technical staff assistance in their use. A listing of Depository Libraries is available through the Government Printing Office. A search of patents can be informative. Besides indicating if your device is patentable, it may disclose patents better than yours, but not in production. You may be able to contact the inventor and arrange to have it manufactured and sold by your company.

Another service provided for inventors by the Patent Office is the acceptance and preservation for a two-year period of the papers disclosing an invention. This "disclosure document" is accepted as evidence of the date of conception of the invention. A fee must accompany the disclosure. It must also be accompanied by a self-addressed, stamped envelope and a duplicate copy signed by the inventor. The papers will be stamped with an identifying number, then returned with the reminder that the disclosure document may be relied upon only as evidence of the date of conception and that an application must be filed in order to provide patent protection. During that time you must show continuous work and demonstrate that you are involved in an "active" as opposed to a "passive" process. This can be accomplished through the use of the journal discussed earlier in this chapter.

An application for a patent is made to the Commissioner of Patents and Trademarks and includes:

1. A written document which comprises a specification (description and claims), and an oath or declaration.

2. A drawing in those cases in which a drawing is necessary.

3. A filing fee according to the fee schedule.

The term of a patent is 17 years. A maintenance fee is due $3\frac{1}{2}$, $7\frac{1}{2}$ and $11\frac{1}{2}$ years after the original grant for all patents issuing from the applications filed on and after December 12, 1980. The maintenance fee must be paid at the stipulated times to maintain the patent in force. After the patent has expired, anyone may make, use or sell the invention without permission of the patentee, provided that matter covered by other unexpired patents is not used.

The preparation of an application for a patent and the proceedings in the Patent and Trademark Office to obtain that patent are undertakings that require a thorough knowledge of the scientific or technical matters involved in the particular invention, as well as knowledge of the legal aspects of the patent process. Although inventors may prepare and file their own applications and may conduct their own proceedings, they may find it difficult. The patent process can be tedious, complicated and lengthy. Most inventors employ the services of registered patent attorneys or patent agents. However, it is to your advantage to be as knowledgeable as possible about the patent process.

Provisional Patent Application

In June of 1995, Congress approved the Provisional Patent Application (PPA), which was designed to allow individual inventors to show their inventions to potential manufacturers and investors without fear of having their ideas stolen. Along with a $75 filing fee, you submit a one-page cover sheet, a declaration statement, informal drawings and a detailed description of the invention. The PPA information is retained in confidence and is automatically abandoned 12 months after filing. It does not replace the need for applying for a regular patent. Before the PPA expires, the applicant must file a nonprovisional application to obtain a patent. For specific details about changes in U.S. patent law and practice, contact the resources listed at the end of this chapter.

Summary

Once you have written, notarized and filed your disclosure letter, have started your journal and explored the possibilities of copyright, trademark and patent, you can begin to disclose your idea to the public.

Resources

Books

Elias, Stephen, *A Dictionary of Patent, Copyright, & Trademark Terms* (Berkeley, CA: Nolo Press, 1991).

Grissom, Fred, and David Pressman, *The Inventor's Notebook* (Berkeley, CA: Nolo Press, 1987).

McGrath, Kate and Stephen Elias, *Trademark: How to Name Your Business and Product*, (Berkeley, CA: Nolo, 1994).

Nicolas, Ted, *How to Get Your Own Trademark* (Chicago: Dearborn Trade, 1992).

Pressman, David, *Patent it Yourself* (Berkeley, CA: Nolo Press, 1991).

Salone, M.J., *How to Copyright Software*, (Berkeley, CA: Nolo Press, 1989).

Young, Woody, *Copyright Law: What You Don't Know Can Hurt You* (San Juan Capistrano, CA: Joy Publishing, 1988).

References

Official Gazette of the U.S. Patent and Trademark Office: Official journal relating to patents and trademarks that is issued each Tuesday in two parts, one describing patents and the other trademarks. Sold by subscription and by single copies by the Superintendent of Documents.

Index of Patents: The annual index to the "Official Gazette" is currently published in two volumes; one an index to patentees and the other an index by subject matter of the patents. Available through the Superintendent of Documents and in public and college libraries.

Index of Trademarks: An annual index of registrants of trademarks, available through the Superintendent of Documents and in public and college libraries.

Agencies

Copyright Office, LM 455
Library of Congress
Washington, DC 20559
(202) 707-3000 (Copyright Information Specialist)
(202) 707-9100 (Forms and circular requests)

Copyright Publications (partial list):

Circular 1: *Copyright Basics*

Circular 2: *Publications on Copyright*
Circular 3: *Copyright Notice*
Circular 22: *How to Investigate the Copyright Status of a Work*
Circular 40: *Copyright Registration for Works of the Visual Arts*
Circular 40a: *Deposit Requirements for Registration of Claims to Copyright in Visual Arts Material*

Copyright Information Kits (partial list). Each copyright information kit contains material on the kit's title and includes circulars, announcements and application forms. They are ordered by kit number:

Kit 109: *Books*
Kit 113: *Computer Programs*
Kit 116: *Copyright Searches*
Kit 108: *Games*
Kit 107: *Photographs*
Kit 121: *Sound Recordings*

U.S. Patent and Trademark Office
Assistant Commissioner for Trademarks
2900 Crystal Drive
Arlington, VA 22202-3513
(703) 557-INFO
(703) 308-4357
(703) 305-9300; Lois Boland, regarding changes in U.S. patent law.
(703) 305-9282; John Gonzales or Magdelan Greenlief, regarding changes in the rules of practice.

Basic Facts about Patents
Basic Information about Trademarks

U.S. Small Business Administration
P.O. Box 46521
Denver, CO 80201
(800) 827-5722 (SBA Small Business Answer Desk)

Avoiding Patent, Trademark and Copyright Problems PI 2...$1.00
Trademarks and Business Goodwill PI 3...$1.00

Superintendent of Documents
P.O. Box 371954
Pittsburgh, PA 15250-7954
(202) 783-3238

General Information Concerning Patents
Patent Attorneys and Agents Registered to Practice Before the U.S. Patent Office

Sample Journal Page

June 23, 1996: Irvine Valley College, Irvine, CA. Took class in Basic Recordkeeping. Met with Instructor, Linda Pinson, regarding consulting and setting up my recordkeeping system.

June 25, 1996: Contacted Dan Jenkins at The Boating Shop regarding teaching basic kayak skills and scheduling demonstrations of the sport. Positive response. We will jointly develop a questionnaire to be distributed to customers in the shop in order to determine interest. (714) 555-7642.

June 28, 1996: Arranged to speak to the Chamber of Commerce on the subject "Kayaking around Baja" on Thursday, August 12, at The Market Restaurant. Contact: Jane Morgan (714) 555-9734.

July 1, 1996: Taught class, "Kayaking Skills" from 7 to 9 P.M. at Anderson Community College, Blairsville. Twenty-seven students attended, ages ranged from 18 to 52, interest from five students regarding an organized Baja trip: Sam Johnson 463-9728, Glenn Smith 743-9652, Sarah Bennett 462-8931, Suzanne Kim 426-9276, David Kelley 626-6201.

July 4, 1996: Exhibited at Community Days in the Park on Beach Street. Approximately 10,000 attended event. Conducted questionnaire interviews with 462 people responding as follows:

1. Previous kayaking experience = 36
   Where: river = 12   ocean = 24
   Did you enjoy?
   Yes = 16 (supervised, safety equipment, skilled leader)
   No = 20 (poorly planned, off schedule, cancelled with no refund)

2. Interest in kayaking classes = 216
   Evenings = 113   Weekday = 26   Saturday = 186

3. What would you expect to pay?
   Range $35-$50 for 4 hr. class $175-$250 for 2 day trip

4. Majority:
   Read *Register* (397)
   Listen to KZLM radio (201)
   Respond to coupons in Penny Saver (122)

July 26, 1996: Talk radio show scheduled with Don Wells on KZLM on Wednesday, August 25 from 5 to 6 P.M. Will discuss past trips, announce classes scheduled, take listener calls.

Copyright Form VA

⚖ Filling Out Application Form VA

Detach and read these instructions before completing this form.
Make sure all applicable spaces have been filled in before you return this form.

BASIC INFORMATION

When to Use This Form: Use Form VA for copyright registration of published or unpublished works of the visual arts. This category consists of "pictorial, graphic, or sculptural works," including two-dimensional and three-dimensional works of fine, graphic, and applied art, photographs, prints and art reproductions, maps, globes, charts, technical drawings, diagrams, and models.

What Does Copyright Protect? Copyright in a work of the visual arts protects those pictorial, graphic, or sculptural elements that, either alone or in combination, represent an "original work of authorship." The statute declares: "In no case does copyright protection for an original work of authorship extend to any idea, procedure, process, system, method of operation, concept, principle, or discovery, regardless of the form in which it is described, explained, illustrated, or embodied in such work."

Works of Artistic Craftsmanship and Designs: "Works of artistic craftsmanship" are registrable on Form VA, but the statute makes clear that protection extends to "their form" and not to "their mechanical or utilitarian aspects." The "design of a useful article" is considered copyrightable "only if, and only to the extent that, such design incorporates pictorial, graphic, or sculptural features that can be identified separately from, and are capable of existing independently of, the utilitarian aspects of the article."

Labels and Advertisements: Works prepared for use in connection with the sale or advertisement of goods and services are registrable if they contain "original work of authorship." Use Form VA if the copyrightable material in the work you are registering is mainly pictorial or graphic; use Form TX if it consists mainly of text. **NOTE:** Words and short phrases such as names, titles, and slogans cannot be protected by copyright, and the same is true of standard symbols, emblems, and other commonly used graphic designs that are in the public domain. When used commercially, material of that sort can sometimes be protected under state laws of unfair competition or under the Federal trademark laws. For information about trademark registration, write to the Commissioner of Patents and Trademarks, Washington, D.C. 20231.

Architectural Works: Copyright protection extends to the design of buildings created for the use of human beings. Architectural works created on or after December 1, 1990, or that on December 1, 1990, were unconstructed and embodied only in unpublished plans or drawings are eligible. Request Circular 41 for more information.

Deposit to Accompany Application: An application for copyright registration must be accompanied by a deposit consisting of copies representing the entire work for which registration is to be made.

Unpublished Work: Deposit one complete copy.

Published Work: Deposit two complete copies of the best edition.

Work First Published Outside the United States: Deposit one complete copy of the first foreign edition.

Contribution to a Collective Work: Deposit one complete copy of the best edition of the collective work.

The Copyright Notice: For works first published on or after March 1, 1989, the law provides that a copyright notice in a specified form "may be placed on all publicly distributed copies from which the work can be visually perceived." Use of the copyright notice is the responsibility of the copyright owner and does not require advance permission from the Copyright Office. The required form of the notice for copies generally consists of three elements: (1) the symbol "©", or the word "Copyright," or the abbreviation "Copr."; (2) the year of first publication; and (3) the name of the owner of copyright. For example: "© 1995 Jane Cole." The notice is to be affixed to the copies "in such manner and location as to give reasonable notice of the claim of copyright." Works first published prior to March 1, 1989, **must** carry the notice or risk loss of copyright protection.

For information about notice requirements for works published before March 1, 1989, or other copyright information, write: Information Section, LM-401, Copyright Office, Library of Congress, Washington, D.C. 20559-6000.

LINE-BY-LINE INSTRUCTIONS
Please type or print using black ink.

1 SPACE 1: Title

Title of This Work: Every work submitted for copyright registration must be given a title to identify that particular work. If the copies of the work bear a title (or an identifying phrase that could serve as a title), transcribe that wording *completely* and *exactly* on the application. Indexing of the registration and future identification of the work will depend on the information you give here. For an architectural work that has been constructed, add the date of construction after the title; if unconstructed at this time, add "not yet constructed."

Previous or Alternative Titles: Complete this space if there are any additional titles for the work under which someone searching for the registration might be likely to look, or under which a document pertaining to the work might be recorded.

Publication as a Contribution: If the work being registered is a contribution to a periodical, serial, or collection, give the title of the contribution in the "Title of This Work" space. Then, in the line headed "Publication as a Contribution," give information about the collective work in which the contribution appeared.

Nature of This Work: Briefly describe the general nature or character of the pictorial, graphic, or sculptural work being registered for copyright. Examples: "Oil Painting"; "Charcoal Drawing"; "Etching"; "Sculpture"; "Map"; "Photograph"; "Scale Model"; "Lithographic Print"; "Jewelry Design"; "Fabric Design."

2 SPACE 2: Author(s)

General Instruction: After reading these instructions, decide who are the "authors" of this work for copyright purposes. Then, unless the work is a "collective work," give the requested information about every "author" who contributed any appreciable amount of copyrightable matter to this version of the work. If you need further space, request Continuation Sheets. In the case of a collective work, such as a catalog of paintings or collection of cartoons by various authors, give information about the author of the collective work as a whole.

Name of Author: The fullest form of the author's name should be given. Unless the work was "made for hire," the individual who actually created the work is its "author." In the case of a work made for hire, the statute provides that "the employer or other person for whom the work was prepared is considered the author."

What is a "Work Made for Hire"? A "work made for hire" is defined as: (1) "a work prepared by an employee within the scope of his or her employment"; or (2) "a work specially ordered or commissioned for use as a contribution to a collective work, as a part of a motion picture or other audiovisual work, as a translation, as a supplementary work, as a compilation, as an instructional text, as a test, as answer material for a test, or as an atlas, if the parties expressly agree in a written instrument signed by them that the work shall be considered a work made for hire." If you have checked "Yes" to indicate that the work was "made for hire," you must give the full legal name of the employer (or other person for whom the work was prepared). You may also include the name of the employee along with the name of the employer (for example: "Elster Publishing Co., employer for hire of John Ferguson").

"Anonymous" or "Pseudonymous" Work: An author's contribution to a work is "anonymous" if that author is not identified on the copies or phonorecords of the work. An author's contribution to a work is "pseudonymous" if that author is identified on the copies or phonorecords under a fictitious name. If the work is "anonymous" you may: (1) leave the line blank; or (2) state "anonymous" on the line; or (3) reveal the author's identity. If the work is "pseudonymous" you may: (1) leave the line blank; or (2) give the pseudonym and identify it as such (for example: "Huntley Haverstock, pseudonym"); or (3) reveal the author's name, making clear which is the real name and which is the pseudonym (for example: "Henry Leek, whose pseudonym is Priam Farrel"). However, the citizenship or domicile of the author **must** be given in all cases.

Dates of Birth and Death: If the author is dead, the statute requires that the year of death be included in the application unless the work is anonymous or pseudonymous. The author's birth date is optional but is useful as a form of identification. Leave this space blank if the author's contribution was a "work made for hire."

Author's Nationality or Domicile: Give the country of which the author is a citizen, or the country in which the author is domiciled. Nationality or domicile **must** be given in all cases.

Copyright Form VA, continued

Nature of Authorship: Catagories of pictorial, graphic, and sculptural authorship are listed below. Check the box(es) that best describe(s) each author's contribution to the work.

3-Dimensional sculptures: fine art sculptures, toys, dolls, scale models, and sculptural designs applied to useful articles.

2-Dimensional artwork: watercolor and oil paintings; pen and ink drawings; logo illustrations; greeting cards; collages; stencils; patterns; computer graphics; graphics appearing in screen displays; artwork appearing on posters, calendars, games, commercial prints and labels, and packaging, as well as 2-dimensional artwork applied to useful articles.

Reproductions of works of art: reproductions of preexisting artwork made by, for example, lithography, photoengraving, or etching.

Maps: cartographic representations of an area such as state and county maps, atlases, marine charts, relief maps, and globes.

Photographs: pictorial photographic prints and slides and holograms.

Jewelry designs: 3-dimensional designs applied to rings, pendants, earrings, necklaces, and the like.

Designs on sheetlike materials: designs reproduced on textiles, lace, and other fabrics; wallpaper; carpeting; floor tile; wrapping paper; and clothing.

Technical drawings: diagrams illustrating scientific or technical information in linear form such as architectural blueprints or mechanical drawings.

Text: textual material that accompanies pictorial, graphic, or sculptural works such as comic strips, greeting cards, games rules, commercial prints or labels, and maps.

Architectural works: designs of buildings, including the overall form as well as the arrangement and composition of spaces and elements of the design. NOTE: Any registration for the underlying architectural plans must be applied for on a separate Form VA, checking the box "Technical drawing."

3 SPACE 3: Creation and Publication

General Instructions: Do not confuse "creation" with "publication." Every application for copyright registration must state "the year in which creation of the work was completed." Give the date and nation of first publication only if the work has been published.

Creation: Under the statute, a work is "created" when it is fixed in a copy or phonorecord for the first time. Where a work has been prepared over a period of time, the part of the work existing in fixed form on a particular date constitutes the created work on that date. The date you give here should be the year in which the author completed the particular version for which registration is now being sought, even if other versions exist or if further changes or additions are planned.

Publication: The statute defines "publication" as "the distribution of copies or phonorecords of a work to the public by sale or other transfer of ownership, or by rental, lease, or lending"; a work is also "published" if there has been an "offering to distribute copies or phonorecords to a group of persons for purposes of further distribution, public performance, or public display." Give the full date (month, day, year) when, and the country where, publication first occurred. If first publication took place simultaneously in the United States and other countries, it is sufficient to state "U.S.A."

4 SPACE 4: Claimant(s)

Name(s) and Address(es) of Copyright Claimant(s): Give the name(s) and address(es) of the copyright claimant(s) in this work even if the claimant is the same as the author. Copyright in a work belongs initially to the author of the work (including, in the case of a work make for hire, the employer or other person for whom the work was prepared). The copyright claimant is either the author of the work or a person or organization to whom the copyright initially belonging to the author has been transferred.

Transfer: The statute provides that, if the copyright claimant is not the author, the application for registration must contain "a brief statement of how the claimant obtained ownership of the copyright." If any copyright claimant named in space 4 is not an author named in space 2, give a brief statement explaining how the claimant(s) obtained ownership of the copyright. Examples: "By written contract"; "Transfer of all rights by author"; "Assignment"; "By will." Do not attach transfer documents or other attachments or riders.

5 SPACE 5: Previous Registration

General Instructions: The questions in space 5 are intended to find out **whether an earlier registration has been made** for this work and, if so, whether

there is any basis for a new registration. As a rule, only one basic copyright registration can be made for the same version of a particular work.

Same Version: If this version is substantially the same as the work covered by a previous registration, a second registration is not generally possible unless: (1) the work has been registered in unpublished form and a second registration is now being sought to cover this first published edition; or (2) someone other than the author is identified as a copyright claimant in the earlier registration, and the author is now seeking registration in his or her own name. If either of these two exceptions apply, check the appropriate box and give the earlier registration number and date. Otherwise, do not submit Form VA; instead, write the Copyright Office for information about supplementary registration or recordation of transfers of copyright ownership.

Changed Version: If the work has been changed and you are now seeking registration to cover the additions or revisions, check the last box in space 5, give the earlier registration number and date, and complete both parts of space 6 in accordance with the instruction below.

Previous Registration Number and Date: If more than one previous registration has been made for the work, give the number and date of the latest registration.

6 SPACE 6: Derivative Work or Compilation

General Instructions: Complete space 6 if this work is a "changed version," "compilation," or "derivative work," and if it incorporates one or more earlier works that have already been published or registered for copyright, or that have fallen into the public domain. A "compilation" is defined as "a work formed by the collection and assembling of preexisting materials or of data that are selected, coordinated, or arranged in such a way that the resulting work as a whole constitutes an original work of authorship." A "derivative work" is "a work based on one or more preexisting works." Examples of derivative works include reproductions of works of art, sculptures based on drawings, lithographs based on paintings, maps based on previously published sources, or "any other form in which a work may be recast, transformed, or adapted." Derivative works also include works "consisting of editorial revisions, annotations, or other modifications" if these changes, as a whole, represent an original work of authorship.

Preexisting Material (space 6a): Complete this space **and** space 6b for derivative works. In this space identify the preexisting work that has been recast, transformed, or adapted. Examples of preexisting material might be "Grunewald Altarpiece" or "19th century quilt design." Do not complete this space for compilations.

Material Added to This Work (space 6b): Give a brief, general statement of the **additional** new material covered by the copyright claim for which registration is sought. In the case of a derivative work, identify this new material. Examples: "Adaptation of design and additional artistic work"; "Reproduction of painting by photolithography"; "Additional cartographic material"; "Compilation of photographs." If the work is a compilation, give a brief, general statement describing both the material that has been compiled **and** the compilation itself. Example: "Compilation of 19th century political cartoons."

7,8,9 SPACE 7,8,9: Fee, Correspondence, Certification, Return Address

Deposit Account: If you maintain a Deposit Account in the Copyright Office, identify it in space 7. Otherwise leave the space blank and send the fee of $20 with your application and deposit.

Correspondence (space 7): This space should contain the name, address, area code, and telephone number of the person to be consulted if correspondence about this application becomes necessary.

Certification (space 8): The application cannot be accepted unless it bears the date and the **handwritten signature** of the author or other copyright claimant, or of the owner of exclusive right(s), or of the duly authorized agent of the author, claimant, or owner of exclusive right(s).

Address for Return of Certificate (space 9): The address box must be completed legibly since the certificate will be returned in a window envelope.

PRIVACY ACT ADVISORY STATEMENT Required by the Privacy Act of 1974 (P.L. 93 - 579)
The authority for requesting this information is title 17, U.S.C., secs. 409 and 410. Furnishing the requested information is voluntary. But if the information is not furnished, it may be necessary to delay or refuse registration and you may not be entitled to certain relief, remedies, and benefits provided in chapters 4 and 5 of title 17, U.S.C.
The principal uses of the requested information are the establishment and maintenance of a public record and the examination of the application for compliance with legal requirements.
Other routine uses include public inspection and copying, preparation of public indexes, preparation of public catalogs of copyright registrations, and preparation of search reports upon request.
NOTE: No other advisory statement will be given in connection with this application. Please keep this statement and refer to it if we communicate with you regarding this application.

Copyright Form VA, continued

FORM VA
For a Work of the Visual Arts
UNITED STATES COPYRIGHT OFFICE

REGISTRATION NUMBER

VA   VAU

EFFECTIVE DATE OF REGISTRATION

Month   Day   Year

DO NOT WRITE ABOVE THIS LINE. IF YOU NEED MORE SPACE, USE A SEPARATE CONTINUATION SHEET.

1

TITLE OF THIS WORK ▼

NATURE OF THIS WORK ▼ See instructions

PREVIOUS OR ALTERNATIVE TITLES ▼

PUBLICATION AS A CONTRIBUTION If this work was published as a contribution to a periodical, serial, or collection, give information about the collective work in which the contribution appeared.   **Title of Collective Work ▼**

If published in a periodical or serial give: Volume ▼   Number ▼   Issue Date ▼   On Pages ▼

2

a

NAME OF AUTHOR ▼

DATES OF BIRTH AND DEATH
Year Born ▼   Year Died ▼

Was this contribution to the work a "work made for hire"?
☐ Yes
☐ No

AUTHOR'S NATIONALITY OR DOMICILE
Name of Country
OR { Citizen of ▶ _____
Domiciled in ▶ _____

WAS THIS AUTHOR'S CONTRIBUTION TO THE WORK
Anonymous? ☐ Yes ☐ No
Pseudonymous? ☐ Yes ☐ No
If the answer to either of these questions is "Yes," see detailed instructions.

NATURE OF AUTHORSHIP Check appropriate box(es). **See instructions**
☐ 3-Dimensional sculpture
☐ 2-Dimensional artwork
☐ Reproduction of work of art
☐ Design on sheetlike material
☐ Map
☐ Photograph
☐ Jewelry design
☐ Technical drawing
☐ Text
☐ Architectural work

NOTE

Under the law, the "author" of a "work made for hire" is generally the employer, not the employee (see instructions). For any part of this work that was "made for hire" check "Yes" in the space provided, give the employer (or other person for whom the work was prepared) as "Author" of that part, and leave the space for dates of birth and death blank.

b

NAME OF AUTHOR ▼

DATES OF BIRTH AND DEATH
Year Born ▼   Year Died ▼

Was this contribution to the work a "work made for hire"?
☐ Yes
☐ No

AUTHOR'S NATIONALITY OR DOMICILE
Name of Country
OR { Citizen of ▶ _____
Domiciled in ▶ _____

WAS THIS AUTHOR'S CONTRIBUTION TO THE WORK
Anonymous? ☐ Yes ☐ No
Pseudonymous? ☐ Yes ☐ No
If the answer to either of these questions is "Yes," see detailed instructions.

NATURE OF AUTHORSHIP Check appropriate box(es). **See instructions**
☐ 3-Dimensional sculpture
☐ 2-Dimensional artwork
☐ Reproduction of work of art
☐ Design on sheetlike material
☐ Map
☐ Photograph
☐ Jewelry design
☐ Technical drawing
☐ Text
☐ Architectural work

3

a YEAR IN WHICH CREATION OF THIS WORK WAS COMPLETED This information must be given _____ ◀Year in all cases.

b DATE AND NATION OF FIRST PUBLICATION OF THIS PARTICULAR WORK
Complete this information ONLY if this work has been published. Month ▶ _____ Day ▶ _____ Year ▶ _____
◀ Nation

4

See instructions before completing this space.

COPYRIGHT CLAIMANT(S) Name and address must be given even if the claimant is the same as the author given in space 2. ▼

TRANSFER If the claimant(s) named here in space 4 is (are) different from the author(s) named in space 2, give a brief statement of how the claimant(s) obtained ownership of the copyright. ▼

APPLICATION RECEIVED

ONE DEPOSIT RECEIVED

TWO DEPOSITS RECEIVED

FUNDS RECEIVED

DO NOT WRITE HERE OFFICE USE ONLY

MORE ON BACK ▶ • Complete all applicable spaces (numbers 5-9) on the reverse side of this page.
• See detailed instructions. • Sign the form at line 8.

DO NOT WRITE HERE
Page 1 of _____ pages

Copyright Form VA, continued

EXAMINED BY	FORM VA
CHECKED BY	

☐ CORRESPONDENCE
Yes

FOR
COPYRIGHT
OFFICE
USE
ONLY

DO NOT WRITE ABOVE THIS LINE. IF YOU NEED MORE SPACE, USE A SEPARATE CONTINUATION SHEET.

PREVIOUS REGISTRATION Has registration for this work, or for an earlier version of this work, already been made in the Copyright Office?

☐ Yes ☐ No If your answer is "Yes," why is another registration being sought? (Check appropriate box) ▼

a. ☐ This is the first published edition of a work previously registered in unpublished form.

b. ☐ This is the first application submitted by this author as copyright claimant.

c. ☐ This is a changed version of the work, as shown by space 6 on this application.

If your answer is "Yes," give: Previous Registration Number ▼   Year of Registration ▼

5

DERIVATIVE WORK OR COMPILATION Complete both space 6a and 6b for a derivative work; complete only 6b for a compilation.

a. Preexisting Material Identify any preexisting work or works that this work is based on or incorporates. ▼

b. Material Added to This Work Give a brief, general statement of the material that has been added to this work and in which copyright is claimed. ▼

6

See instructions
before completing
this space.

DEPOSIT ACCOUNT If the registration fee is to be charged to a Deposit Account established in the Copyright Office, give name and number of Account.
Name ▼   Account Number ▼

7

CORRESPONDENCE Give name and address to which correspondence about this application should be sent.   Name/Address/Apt/City/State/ZIP ▼

Area Code and Telephone Number ▶

Be sure to
give your
daytime phone
◀ number

CERTIFICATION* I, the undersigned, hereby certify that I am the

check only one ▼

☐ author

☐ other copyright claimant

☐ owner of exclusive right(s)

☐ authorized agent of ————————————————————
Name of author or other copyright claimant, or owner of exclusive right(s) ▲

8

of the work identified in this application and that the statements made
by me in this application are correct to the best of my knowledge.

Typed or printed name and date ▼ If this application gives a date of publication in space 3, do not sign and submit it before that date.

Date ▶ ————————————————

☞   Handwritten signature (X) ▼

Mail certificate to:	Name ▼	**YOU MUST:** • Complete all necessary spaces • Sign your application in space 8
	Number/Street/Apt ▼	**SEND ALL 3 ELEMENTS IN THE SAME PACKAGE:** 1. Application form 2. Nonrefundable $20 filing fee in check or money order payable to *Register of Copyrights* 3. Deposit material
Certificate will be mailed in window envelope	City/State/ZIP ▼	**MAIL TO:** Register of Copyrights Library of Congress Washington, D.C. 20559-6000

9

The Use of Questionnaires

Because marketing is a dynamic process, you must find a cost effective method of keeping up with the changes occurring within the marketplace. A previous section helped you identify products and services that are compatible with current trends. You now want to get a response from the public regarding the product or service you are interested in providing. Before you invest time and money in developing your idea, determine whether a need or desire for it exists in the buying community. Surveys are an excellent means of determining the response to what you have to offer. A questionnaire is the most common means of collecting data.

Survey: A research method in which people are asked questions.

Format

In formulating a questionnaire, care must be given to the structure, word choice and sequence of the questions. Determine what you need to know, then choose your questions. Wording is important; be simple, unbiased and direct. Be aware of the sequence of your questions. The first question should generate interest.

Questionnaire: A data-gathering form used to collect information by a personal interview, with a telephone survey or through the mail.

A questionnaire begins with an introduction. Establish your initial contact with the reader in the opening statement. Tell just enough about the nature of your survey to arouse interest. Point out that you value the reader's response. We all like to feel that our opinions are important.

Next, you will begin work on the body of the questionnaire by making a list of the information you need. Don't worry about phrasing or order at this point. Get everything down on paper, then go back and develop your wording and sequence. There are three types of questions and they vary according to structure and response.

Open-Ended Questions

This type of question requires the respondent to provide the reply. Choices are not given; the respondent must fill in the blanks. These are considered qualitative questions because they allow the person being surveyed to express an opinion in words. This type of question often gathers the most subjective information.

Multiple-Choice Questions

Choice: A decision to purchase that is based on an evaluation of alternatives.

You provide the respondent with a selection of answers. One example would be yes-or-no-type questions; there are only two responses. There is little chance of a biased answer. Some questions will warrant more choices. When using multiple-choice questions, run different copies of the questionnaire and vary the order in which the choices appear following the question. People tend to select an answer from the front of the list and your results may be biased. If the question requires the respondent to choose an answer from a numerical list, there is a tendency to select an answer from the middle of the list. People wish to appear "average" or "normal" and assume that choices at either end of the range reflect extremes.

Rating Questions

These are sometimes called value-judgment questions. The respondent is asked to reflect an opinion on a ranking scale; for example, a scale of one to ten. If a ranking scale is used, be sure to indicate the value of the number range, i.e.: one is equal to the least and ten is equal to the most.

Try to phrase your questions so they are clear and easily understood. Choose language that is appropriate to the group who will be responding. Use terms that are familiar to the consumer. Avoid words or phrases that are unique to your industry and not in common usage.

Ask questions in a logical sequence. Questions in a subject area should be grouped together. The first question creates interest. Begin with general questions and build to the more specific. Ask the most difficult or involved questions at the end. They will be turn-offs if they appear early in the questionnaire. Since respondents will have completed most of the work by the time they get to the more involved questions, they will be less apt to abandon the project.

The questionnaire ends with the basic data: the name, address and phone number of the respondent. Often a more honest and subjective response will result if providing this information is optional. Many questionnaire respondents prefer to remain anonymous.

Types of Information

A well-designed questionnaire can gather data covering four main areas: interest in your product or service, data on demographics, methods for reaching the market and information on the competition.

Questions aimed at determining a need for your product or service.

1. Do you like to play card and/or board games?

2. Do you own a personal computer?

3. In the past two months, how many times have you eaten take-out food?

4. Would you be interested in take-out, "home-cooked" food?

5. Do you have an interest in environmental health issues?

Questions that indicate the type of lifestyle of the prospects.

1. Do you work away from your home city?

2. Do you shop where you work?

3. Do you shop where you live?

4. Would you be interested in home delivery or in-home service?

5. Into which of these age groups do you fall?

6. What is your occupation?

7. Do you own or rent your home?

8. What is your household income?

9. How much would you expect to pay for this product or service?

Questions that show you how to reach the respondents.

1. What newspapers do you read?

2. What section do you read first?

3. What radio stations do you listen to?

4. What television programs do you regularly watch?

5. Which magazines do you read?

6. Do you use discount coupons?

7. In the last six months, how many times did you order a product from a catalog?

8. Where would you expect to buy this product?

Questions about the competition.

1. What company do you currently use?

2. Are you satisfied with its product or service?

3. How could that product or service be improved to meet your needs?

4. What take-out food do you currently eat?

5. Are you satisfied with that food?

6. If not, how could it be improved?

7. What do you currently pay for this product or service?

These example questions are in a simple format to give you an idea of the type of information you can gather in each category. Refer to the previous section on format when structuring your own questions. Sample questionnaires have been included at the end of this chapter (see pps. 32, 33 and 34).

Discount: A deduction from the stated or list price of a product or service.

Distribution

Decide who is to be surveyed, how many people are to be contacted and how they will be reached. They can be contacted by mail, telephone, personal or group interview. Questionnaires must be distributed to potential customers for their results to be valid. Don't give them to friends and family and expect results that reflect your market.

Direct Mail

Unfortunately, the mail as a market research vehicle has been overused and you must extend some courtesies to increase your response rate. Include a self-addressed, stamped envelope in all of your mailings to encourage the recipient to return the questionnaire. Offer discount coupons. Some entrepreneurs are increasing the response rate by enclosing a dollar bill in each mailing accompanied by a note thanking the respondent for taking the time to complete the form. There is a moral obligation to respond! Hand address the envelopes. This takes time, but has proven to increase the response rate. Metered mail is a turn-off; use stamps for a personalized impression.

Carefully choose your sampling group. This can be done most effectively by renting a mailing list from a list broker (look under "Mailing Lists" in the yellow page section of your telephone book). Note that you will **rent** the list. Most mailing lists are rented for one-time use. A small percentage of the names on your list will be employees of the list company. They will log in your mailing. If they receive a second piece of literature from you, the list company will check to see if you have rented for a second mailing. If you are reusing a one-time rental, you may be denied future rentals. Anyone who responds to your mailing becomes your customer, and you can send out repeat mailings to that individual. The company employees do not respond to offers.

Your study of trends and your ultimate choice of a product or service to research will give you some clues as to prospective customers. The list broker can prepare a list according to the information that you give regarding age, occupation, sex, buying habits, education, interests, family status, income and geographic location. Get a feeling for who you think will be interested, rent a list, send out your questionnaire and see if the results agree with your original assessment.

The more specific and narrow you make your list, the more you will have to pay per name. You will pay more for a list targeting high-income professionals who live in Beverly Hills, eat out three or more times per

Direct mail: Marketing goods or services directly to the consumer through the mail.

week, are married with no children and own BMWs, than for a list of high income, married residents of Beverly Hills. A more specific list could be cost-effective in the long run if it helps you clearly define your market.

Telemarketing

Telephone surveys are another means of gathering data. This medium is also being overused; consumers are increasingly unwilling to take calls from strangers who are conducting surveys.

You may wish to have the survey done for you by a telemarketing survey company. Research firms have specially trained people who may have more success in getting a response. Even if you have an outside agency conduct the study, you can still make recommendations regarding the questions asked.

If you decide to do your own telemarketing survey, make use of your original questionnaire. Prepare a good introduction: "I am calling a few people in your neighborhood for an important and quick survey. I hope you will take a moment to tell me how you feel about _____." Then refer to your questionnaire to gather the information you need. The phone company can provide a directory of geographical listings so you can target any area.

Personal Interviews

Some shopping centers and malls will allow you to canvass shoppers. Be sure to check with the center's management regarding their policy. Dress in a business-like manner and carry a clipboard to hold your questionnaires. Talking to shoppers can be a valuable learning experience. Be aware of shopping patterns. The market segment you interview on Tuesday morning will be quite different from the segment represented by Saturday afternoon shoppers.

You may be able to set up a display table at a fair, art show or similar community event. Have some folding chairs available so you can conduct interviews and get questionnaire responses.

You may wish to hire interviewers to do the work for you. You can hire students, temporary help from agencies or professional interviewers listed in the yellow pages. Be sure to contact local agencies regarding any tax liability you may incur through hiring part-time casual labor.

Group Interviews

Contact local clubs and organizations to see if you can make a presentation on your new product or service. You can offer a donation to the group's treasury in return for the opportunity to present your case. A group discussion may give you some insight into potential problem areas. Hand out your questionnaires or present the questions for discussion. Be aware of the types of people present. Clubs are usually composed of people with similar tastes. There may be a dominant person who is capable of swaying the others. Your results may be biased, but the experience will still provide valuable information.

You may choose to hire a marketing research firm which will have interviewers on its staff. These companies are listed in the yellow page section of your phone directory.

Evaluation of the Response

Plan your strategy for evaluation while you are developing your questionnaire. Use an **address code** on all of your mailings. For example, if your mailing address is 216 Main Street, code your return address by adding Suite 206 or Dept. 1093. Suite 206 could be the code for mailings sent to a specific area. If the questionnaires are returned unsigned, you will still be able to have an idea of the geographical area responding. "Department 1096" could refer to a mailing sent in October of 1996. Use as many codes as you feel you need. You may color code your mailings. Print your questionnaires on different colors or different types of paper. Again, you will have a clear picture of the response from an area.

Use the same basic questionnaire in your research for comparable results. Then you can form a composite from your telephone, personal and group interviews and your questionnaire results.

When you have compiled the data, view it objectively. Because marketing is a dynamic process, you must be flexible regarding your results. Perhaps your original product or service idea wasn't well received. Did the survey point the way to a modification of your idea that would better serve your market?

Sample Questionnaires (pp. 32, 33, 34), a Coding Log (p. 35), and a Marketing Research Worksheet (p. 36) follow this section.

Resources

Books

Bangs, David H., Jr., *Creating Customers* (Chicago: Upstart Publishing Co., 1992).

Bangs, David H., Jr., *The Market Planning Guide, 4th edition* (Chicago: Upstart Publishing Co., 1995).

Breen, George, and A.B. Blankenship, *Do-it-Yourself Market Research* (New York: McGraw-Hill, 1989).

Hall, Stephen, *From Kitchen to Market* (Chicago: Upstart Publishing Co., 1992).

Levinson, Jay Conrad, *Guerrilla Marketing Weapons* (New York: Penguin, 1990).

Mosley, Thomas, *Marketing Your Invention* (Chicago: Upstart Publishing Co., 1992).

Philips, Michael, and Salli Rasberry, *Marketing without Advertising* (Berkeley, CA: Nolo Press, 1990).

Sandhusen, Richard, *Marketing* (Hauppauge, New York: Barron's Educational Series, 1987). Excellent section on questionnaire design and information processing.

References

Encyclopedia of Associations. Reference book published by Gale Research, Detroit, MI.

National Trade and Professional Associations of the U.S. Reference book published by Columbia Books, Washington, DC.

Trade and professional associations often rent their mailing lists.

Agencies

Direct Marketing Association
1120 Avenue of the Americas
New York, NY 10036
(212) 768-7277

Studies consumer and business attitudes toward direct mail and related direct marketing information.

National Mail Order Association
2807 Polk Street NE
Minneapolis, MN 55418
(612) 788-1673

Provides low cost help to small businesses wishing to market through mail order and direct mail. Subscriptions to two monthly newsletters are included in membership fee.

R. L. Polk
431 Howard Street
Detroit, MI 48231
(313) 961-9470

Rents direct mail lists.

Sample Questionnaire: Profile
Marketing Survey for Ocean Adventure

Date _____

Location _____

(Demographic and psychographic information)
Please circle answers:

Male   Female   Single   Married   Other

Age: 18 to 25   26 to 35   36 to 45   46 and over

Your Occupation/Profession _____

Do you enjoy outdoor activities? ____ Yes ____ No

Do you enjoy ocean and beach activities? ____ Yes ____ No

Do you go boating? ____ Yes ____ No

(Information to determine interest and to learn about the competition)
Have you ever been in a kayak? ____ Yes ____ No

If yes:
    a) What did you think of the experience?
    b) Where did you kayak?
    c) Were instructors/guides present?
    d) Did you enjoy the experience?
    e) Would you be interested in classes on kayaking?
    f) Would you be interested in kayaking trips?

If no:
    a) Would you be interested in kayaking lessons?

(Information on reaching the potential market)
Do you use discount coupons? ____ Yes ____ No

What newspapers do you read? _____

What magazines do you read? _____

Have you heard of **OCEAN ADVENTURE**? ____ Yes ____ No

If yes, source _____

Thank you for your response. The following information is helpful to my study but is optional:

Name _____

Address _____

City _____ State _____ Zip _____

Phone (_____)_____

Sample Questionnaire: Product

I am developing a new product and am contacting a few people in your neighborhood for an important and quick survey. I hope you will take a moment to tell me how you feel about board games.

1. Do you play any board games? ____ Yes ____ No
   (If NO, please go to #7)

2. What is your favorite board game?
   ____ Backgammon ____ Checkers ____ Pictionary® ____ Life®
   ____ Clue® ____ Monopoly® ____ Sorry® ____ Other

3. On the average, how often do you play board games?
   ____ Less than once per month ____ Once per month
   ____ Twice per month ____ Once per week ____ More than once per week

4. Would you consider playing a new board game about the stock market?
   ____ Yes ____ No ____ Maybe ____ I don't know

5. How much would you pay for a board game about the stock market?
   ____$6.00 to $10.00 ____$10.01 to $15.00 ____$15.01 to $20.00 ____ Over $20.00

6. What is the first word that comes to mind when you think of the stock
   market? _____

7. On the average, how many hours of television do you watch per week?
   ____ Less than one hour ____1 to 3 hours ____3 to 6 hours ____6 to 9 hours ____9 hours or more

8. Do you clip coupons from the newspaper? ____ Yes ____ No

9. What radio station do you listen to most often? _____

10. What is your age group?
    ____18 to 24 years ____25 to 34 years ____35 to 44 years ____45 to 54 years ____ Over 55 years

11. What is your average household income?
    ___ Under $25,000 ___$25,000 to $45,000 ___$45,000 to $60,000 ___ Over $60,000

Thank you for your response. The following information is helpful to my study but is optional:

Name _____

Address _____

City _____ State _____ Zip _____

Phone (_____)_____

Sample Questionnaire: Service

I am developing a new service and am contacting a few people in your neighborhood for an important and quick survey. I hope you will take a moment to tell me how you feel about take-out food.

1. Do you order take-out food? ____ Yes ____ No

2. What is your favorite take-out food? ____ Chinese food ____ Mexican food ____ Pizza ____ Deli food ____ Burgers ____ Other

3. On the average, how often do you order take-out food? ____ Less than once a month ____ Once a month ____ Twice per month ____ Once per week ____ More than once per week

4. Would you consider full-course take-out meals? ____ Yes ____ No

5. Would you consider home-delivered meals? ____ Yes ____ No

6. How much would you be willing to pay for a full course, home-delivered meal? ____$10.00 ____$15.00 ____$17.50 ____$20.00

7. What is the first word that comes into your mind when you think of full course, home-delivered meals? _____

8. On a scale of one to five, with five signifying very important, please rank the following items as they relate to your feelings about take-out food: (Please circle)

   Containers............... 1 2 3 4 5
   Combinations of foods offered... 1 2 3 4 5
   Temperature when delivered...... 1 2 3 4 5
   Taste.......................... 1 2 3 4 5
   Delivery time.................. 1 2 3 4 5

9. Do you clip coupons from the newspaper? ____ Yes ____ No

10. What newspaper do you read? _____

11. What is your age group? ____18 to 24 years ____25 to 34 years ____35 to 44 years ____45 to 54 years ____ Over 55 years

12. What is your average household income? ___ Under $25,000 ___$25,000 to $45,000 ___$45,000 to $60,000 ___ Over $60,000

Thank you for your response. The following information is helpful to my study but is optional:

Name _____

Address _____

City _____ State _____ Zip _____

Phone (_____)_____

Questionnaire Coding Log
Ocean Adventure

Code	Date	No. Sent	Destination/Recipient	Response Rate	Evaluation
Blue paper	1/5/96	500	Wed. 10 A.M. 1 P.M. Shoppers at Fishermans Wharf Mall	20 interviews 36 returned by mail	6 follow-up for classes/trips 30 follow-up for classes/trips
Yellow paper	1/8/96	500	Sat. 10 A.M. 1 P.M. Shoppers at Fishermans Wharf Mall	52 interviews 160 returned by mail	20 follow-up for classes/trips 52 follow-up
Dept. 196	1/10/96	1000	Mailing list #132, 18-35 yrs., Live in 10 mile radius, $35,000 avg. income	2/1/96—120 returned	26 follow-up for classes/trips
Suite 296	2/7/96	500	Mailing list—local university students	3/1/96—287 returned	158 follow-up for classes/trips
Dept. 296	2/10/96	1000	Mailing list #132 Repeat rental	3/1/96—261 returned	57 follow-up for classes/trips

By analyzing the questionnaire results, the owner of Ocean Adventure can determine that the Saturday shoppers at the Fisherman's Wharf Mall are more responsive. He will analyze their questionnaires in order to get a composite of demographic information. The mailing to university students got a good response and this group will likely form a good part of the target market. The response to the 1/10 and 2/10 mailings indicates the value of repeat mailings to the same group. Through the mailings, the business owner has developed his own mailing list of names of 349 individuals interested in kayaking trips and classes.

Market Research Worksheet
Stock Market Board Game

Questions	Information Source	Results	Effect on Plan
How much would you pay for a board game?	Mail list—10% response. Questionnaire: Mall Tues A.M. Sat P.M. Town Fair	avg. $12.00 avg. $11.00 avg. $15.00 avg. $12.00	$12 -13 range acceptable for market. Will adjust costs to keep selling price within this range.
What is your favorite board game?	Mail list Questionnaires	Backgammon 26 Monopoly 43 Pictionary 86 Clue 13 Trivial Pursuit 82	Indicates that player participation, strategy, skill are important. Will incorporate these elements into game and use as key words in ads.
What is your average household income?	Mail list Questionnaire: Mall Tues A.M. Sat P.M. Town Fair	Majority: 25,000 - 45,000 under 25,000 45,000 - 60,000 25,000 - 45,000	Avg. household income in 25,000 to 45,000 range. Finds $12-13 price acceptable. Will rent mail list using this factor.
What is your age group?	Mail list Questionnaire: Mall Tues a.m. Sat a.m. Town Fair	Majority: 25-34 yrs. 25-34 yrs. 35-44 yrs. 35-44 yrs.	Most responses fall within 25-44 age range. Will use this factor in mail list rental.

Testing the Market

If your questionnaire results have indicated a positive response to your new idea, you will want to proceed with some test marketing of your new product or service. It is much more reliable to judge a potential customer's reaction to a product or service by observing the reaction to an actual sample of your work.

The results of your telephone, personal and group interviews and your questionnaire responses should have defined a group interested in what you have to offer. Go back to that group for your test marketing.

Prototype

Make up a sample of your product. This **prototype** will enable you to analyze the cost involved in manufacturing the item. You will see the time and energy needed for production. You may get an indication of design or material changes which can reduce costs. The prototype is the link between your idea and the final version. It is the refining stage.

Your prototype will depend upon the nature of your product. There are three prototype categories:

1. **Mock-up:** A mock-up is a nonfunctional representation of your product intended to show basic design, size, and color in a three-dimensional form. Since you want to demonstrate the final product, a nonfunctional mock-up will not be adequate for mechanical projects.

2. **Working model:** A working model is made from different materials but is completely functional. It can be handled and can be used in demonstrations.

3. **Production model:** A production model is made of the same materials, is the same size and performs the same function as the final product.

Depending upon your time, talent, financial resources and the complexity of the project, you can produce the prototype yourself or pay someone else to make it. Companies specializing in this service can be found listed in the yellow page section of the phone directory under "Designers - Industrial" or "Designers - Product." College industrial design departments may also be of assistance in building functioning models. A prototype is essential to the market research of a product.

Testing a Product

You are ready to take your idea, in the form of a prototype or the actual product, into the real world. With actual models, potential customers can see how your idea has been transformed into a tangible product. There are advertising agencies and market research firms who will conduct studies for you. Many entrepreneurs find these services too costly. You may choose to do your own test marketing.

Entrepreneur: An innovator of business enterprise who recognizes opportunities to introduce a new product, a new process or an improved organization.

Your research targeted a certain group as potential buyers of your product. Approach that group with the "real thing." By forming small focus groups, you can get reactions to the overall product, to specific features, to its packaging, and to its instructional information. Allow your group to use the product and ask them questions. Negative responses can work for you. Is it easy to use? How can the product be changed to make it more acceptable? Is the instructional information easy to understand? Try different types of packaging. Feedback will give you insight into your final packaging design.

For example, if you are developing a newsletter on environmental issues, print the newsletter on different colors and types of paper. Change the format and type style. Get feedback from your group regarding readability and acceptance, as well as content. If you have developed a new board or card game, gather a group to play the game. Are your rules too complicated or unclear? Print the game using different colors and materials and see which are most acceptable. If you are testing take-out, "home-cooked" foods, experiment with packaging. Do consumers prefer Styrofoam® or cardboard containers? What combinations of foods are most acceptable?

Contact service organizations and clubs about the possibility of presenting a group participation program on what you are offering. Discuss your newsletter and hand out samples. Present your game and have the group play a few rounds, or provide your "home-cooked" foods as the menu for the group's next luncheon or dinner meeting. Be sure to have evaluation sheets prepared and available to get written as well as verbal responses.

Testing a Service

Products can be examined before their use and they can be visually compared to the offerings of the competition. A focus group can handle and read the newsletter. They can look at and play the board game. Consumers have something tangible to show for their money.

Test marketing a service is a challenge. There are fewer reference points for the comparison or evaluation of services. Services are "consumed" as they are provided. Services rely on the people who provide them and therefore offer much more variety.

The best way to test a service is to provide that service and then evaluate the response. Approach your targeted group. If you are starting a house cleaning service, offer four hours of service in return for an evaluation and a letter of recommendation. If you will be adding home delivery to your "home-cooked" food line, provide some complimentary meals. Ask the recipients if the temperature, food variety and taste are acceptable. Look for feedback which will help you to develop your service into one that will be well-received by your customers.

Letters of Reference

When using endorsements or testimonials from customers, be sure to follow the guidelines set forth by the Federal Trade Commission regarding truth in advertising. Endorsements and testimonials must be based on actual use of the product or service. You may be required by the FTC to submit evidence to substantiate the claims.

In order to be valid, a letter of reference or endorsement must be prepared by the actual consumer and must contain a clause giving you permission to use the statements in your advertising and promotion. Keep these letters on file and be prepared to produce them if asked to verify your claims.

While studying trends, developing and protecting your idea, and evaluating your test marketing responses, you have become aware of the competition. The next chapter will give you insights regarding evaluation of that competition.

Resources

Books

Bobrow, Edwin E., *Pioneering New Products: A Market Survival Guide* (Homewood, IL: Dow Jones-Irwin, 1987).

Sandhusen, Richard, *Marketing* (Hauppauge, NY: Barron's Educational Series, 1987).

References

Assael, Henry, *Marketing: Principles & Strategy* (Orlando, FL: Holt, Rinehart, and Winston, 1990).**

McCarthy, E. Jerome and William Perreault, *Basic Marketing* (Homewood, IL: Irwin Publishing, 1987).**

**College textbooks that contain good sections on product development and testing.

Agencies

Bureau of Consumer Protection
Division of Special Statutes
6th Street & Pennsylvania Ave., NW
Washington, DC 20580

Request information on product labeling requirements.

Consumer Products Safety Commission
Bureau of Compliance
5401 Westbard Avenue
Bethesda, MD 20207
(800) 638-2772 (Recorded message tape)

Request information and booklets on laws and regulations regarding product design, such as the following:

The Federal Hazardous Substances Act
Consumer Product Safety Act of 1972
The Flammable Fabrics Act

U.S. Department of Commerce
Office of Consumer Affairs
Washington, DC 20233

Request booklets such as:

Consumer Product Safety

Federal Trade Commission
Office of Consumer Affairs
Washington, DC 20233

Request trade practice rules and labeling requirements that apply to your business or product line.

Food and Drug Administration
5600 Fishers Lane
Rockville, MD 20857

Contact on a federal, state and local level to determine requirements governing the labeling of food-related products.

National Institute of Standards & Technology
U.S. Department of Commerce
Gaithersburg, MD 20899

Write for information on special labeling required for products containing precious metals.

Superintendent of Documents
P.O. Box 371954
Pittsburgh, PA 15250-7954

Request listing of publications such as:

Decision Points in Developing New Products
Inventory Management - Manufacturing/Service

U.S. Fish & Wildlife Service
Division of Law Enforcement
Department of the Interior
Washington, DC 20240

Write for guidelines and restrictions if your product or service involves work with feathers, bones, or endangered species, such as:

FWS 069 - *Federal Laws Restricting Commerce in Wildlife*

Evaluating the Competition

Direct competition will be a business offering the same product or service to the same market. **Indirect competition** is a company with the same product or service but a different market. You may both manufacture the same item, but the other company offers the product for sale through mail order while yours will be available through a retail outlet. Your service may be provided through a mobile unit while the competition provides the same service in a shop. Evaluate both direct and indirect competition.

In a retail business, the toughest competition generally comes from established stores and wholesalers that can offer lower prices because of higher sales volume. In the service industry, strong competition comes from established businesses that have a loyal clientele. Examine the extent and nature of the competition in terms of location, product or service, pricing, methods of distribution, packaging and source of supply.

Look for the strengths and weaknesses of your competitors. You need to identify your competitor's image. To what part of the market does he or she appeal? Can you appeal to the same market in a better way? Or can you discover an untapped market?

Finding the Competition

If your original questionnaire contained questions regarding current service businesses and products used by your market, you will have a head start. Perhaps your individual and group interviews gave you some insight.

The business listings in your telephone directory can provide a wide variety of useful information. The total listing in your business category will give you an idea of the range of your competition. You will be able to pinpoint their locations within your geographical area. Analyze the type and style of each ad. What image do you have of the business based solely on your reaction to the ad? When you make an inspection trip to the place of business, do you retain that same image?

The chamber of commerce can give you a wealth of information on business in general and your business area in particular for the region that you wish to investigate.

National trade and professional associations publish newsletters and magazines that not only predict trends, but also tell about current business. Directories that list these associations are available in the library. Identify those in your field, write to them on your letterhead, and request sample copies of their publications and membership information.

When you have compiled a list of competitors, plan to visit each one. Make copies of the Competition Evaluation Form (see p. 49) at the end of this chapter. Use them to help you gather the data you need.

Evaluating the Competitive Service

The most effective way to evaluate a competitive service is to pose as a customer. Call and ask for job rates, delivery schedules, terms of payment, discount policies, and warranties or guarantees. For example, if you are starting a housecleaning service, find out the minimum number of hours for which you can hire the service. If the minimum service is four hours, is there a market among apartment and condominium dwellers for a weekly two-hour service? Does the homeowner supply cleaning materials? Would your customers appreciate your providing and using a more powerful commercial vacuum? If you are pursuing the idea of home delivery of take-out foods, how do existing businesses handle this? How much time passes between order receipt and delivery?

What was your overall reaction after your phone call to the competition? Do you have confidence in the company? Were you treated in a courteous manner? Were you put on hold and forced to listen to inane music or a series of ads? Your reactions will reflect those of the buying public.

Visit your competitor's place of business. Rate the personnel. Is service prompt and efficient? A colleague who was interested in opening a dry cleaning establishment parked outside one competitor's shop at 7:30 A.M. The shop was due to open at 8:00 A.M. During the time prior to opening, seven customers arrived only to find the business closed. The entrepreneur saw a need for opening a dry cleaners at 7:30 A.M. in order to reach that segment of the market that was being overlooked. Park outside the take-out food establishment we mentioned earlier. When are the peak ordering times? How many drivers are needed? You will get an idea of the volume of business.

Now make use of the competitor's service. Was the housecleaning acceptable? What could be improved? Order the take-out food. Was it delivered in the estimated time frame and was it still hot?

Your analysis of this information on the competition will help you plan your own market entry.

Evaluating a Competitive Product

Visit shops where products similar to yours are displayed. Is the personnel knowledgeable? In our board or card game example, visit a game store. Ask a sales clerk to explain a game similar to yours. If the explanation isn't enough to encourage you to buy the merchandise, you may decide to put a good, thorough description on your game box. Your own packaging may be what will sell the merchandise, not the sales clerk. How are the games displayed and what are their price ranges?

Visit the shop at different times on different days of the week. You will begin to get an idea of traffic flow patterns. Watch the displays of similar products. Do the products seem to be moving? How soon are they marked down or moved to the sale table? Most stores **keystone,** or double the wholesale cost, so you can get an estimate of what your competitors' wholesale prices may be.

Keystone: Setting a retail price at twice the wholesale price.

Wholesale: Selling for resale.

We've referred to the environmental newsletter in our examples. Request samples of similar newsletters. Examine type styles, paper quality and text content. How often are they published? What is the rate for a subscription? Do they include ads to help offset publishing costs?

These examples will give you guidelines in developing your own techniques for competition evaluation. Gather data and draw conclusions about your own competition.

Uniqueness and Benefit to the Customer

As you evaluate your competition, strengths and weaknesses will appear. You will bring the strengths of the competition to your business and you will learn from their weaknesses. The weaknesses are your inroads to success. They point the way toward what will be **unique** about your business. They will help you target what will **benefit your customer**.

The entrepreneur who observed the seven customers who were turned away from the dry cleaning establishment between 7:30 and 8:00 A.M. found a way to be unique. That business owner will benefit customers by opening at 7:30 A.M.

The game maker discovered a need for a clear explanation on the cover of the game box. The customer is benefited by knowing the basic idea of the game and the skill level required for play.

A tree trimmer in San Francisco advertises that he "puts down mats to protect your sod." We get a mental image of a tree surgeon who cares about our lawn and won't let falling limbs gouge holes in it. It doesn't matter that most of these businesses provide this service. He is capitalizing on it to make his mat placement unique and a benefit to his customers.

Analyze advertising with a critical eye and you will begin to see a pattern. We all use shampoo to get our hair clean, but no shampoo company states that its product will get your hair "clean." It will get your hair "cleaner," make it "more manageable," or has a "fresher scent." Find what is unique about your product or service and how that uniqueness will benefit your customers. This uniqueness will be stressed to develop your identity and to prepare you to take on the competition.

Your new product or service may be a monopoly. If successful, you can be certain that competition will follow. In order to remain competitive, you must evaluate the competition throughout the lifetime of your business.

Now that you have determined that there is a need for what you have to offer and have analyzed the competition in terms of how they are filling that need, you are ready to define your target market (your customers).

Resources

Library References for Locating Information on Companies

Is the company publicly owned or is it privately owned/closely held?

1. *Directory of Companies Required to File Annual Reports with the SEC.*

Does the company have a parent company or subsidiaries?

1. *Directory of Corporate Affiliations.*

2. *International Directory of Corporate Affiliations.*

3. *America's Corporate Families.*

Do you need to know the company's type of business, executive officers, number of employees, annual sales?

1. *Standard & Poor's Register of Corporations.*

2. *Dun and Bradstreet's Million Dollar Directory.*

3. *Ward's Business Directory of Largest U.S. Companies.*

4. *Career Guide: Dun's Employment Opportunities Directory.*

5. *Standard Directory of Advertisers.*

Do you need the company's corporate background and financial data?

1. *Standard & Poor's Corporate Records.*

2. *Moody's Manuals.*

3. *Walker's Manual of Western Corporations.*

Is the company newsworthy?

1. *Predicasts F&S Index.*

2. *Business Periodicals Index.*

Is the company listed in a specialized directory?

1. *Thomas Register of American Manufacturers.*

2. *Best's Insurance Reports.*

3. *Standard Directory of Advertising Agencies.*

4. *U.S.A. Oil Industry Directory.*

5. *Who's Who in Electronics.*

6. *Fairchild's Financial Manual of Retail Stores.*

7. *World Aviation Directory.*

8. *Medical and Healthcare Marketplace Guide.*

How does the company rank in the industry?

1. Annual issues of *Fortune, Forbes, Business Week.*

2. *Dun's Business Rankings.*

 NOTE: Contact the reference librarian in the Business Section of your community or college library for availability and use of these references. Many libraries offer computer services and data bases to expand the resources available to you.

Finding Your Target Market

You are going to identify the market segment or group of customers that you can serve profitably based on the size of that market, the resources needed, and the strengths and weaknesses of your business. You don't want to become too big, too soon and not be able to meet deadlines and production schedules. Your goal is to develop a profile of your customers. This profile is formed based on demographic and psychographic information.

Demographics

Markets are described in terms of demographics: age, sex, ethnic background, education, occupation, income, family status and geographic location. Based upon your observations while analyzing the competition and your results from evaluating your questionnaires, you have developed a profile of your customers. You now want to find more customers who will fit this profile.

The information you need is available in census reports published by the Department of Commerce, in directories available in the reference section of the library and in data available through the chambers of commerce and Economic Development Departments.

Population size is one of several factors you will use to help you determine the size of the market. A study of population tables in the **Statistical Abstract of the United States** (reference material published

Psychographics: The system of explaining market behavior in terms of attitudes and life-styles.

51

by the Department of Commerce) will show population shifts. When studied, trends begin to emerge.

There is a shift of the more affluent city dwellers to suburban communities. This requires an adjustment on the part of business. Where does your market live? Where do they work? Do they shop where they live or where they work? If your potential customers shop where they work and work in another city, it will do no good to offer your product or service to them during normal working hours in the city of their residence.

The major population areas of the Middle Atlantic and the East-North Central Regions are continuing to grow. Population is expanding in the Mountain and Pacific areas. The Sun Belt area is a region of rapid growth, primarily because of the increased number of retirees. Trends indicate a movement away from farms and to urban areas.

It is also useful to know the trends in **age distribution**. In the mid-1980s, the number of people age 65 or over surpassed the number of teenagers. This gap has continued to widen as we move into the late 1990s. The response by business to this trend is substantial. Ads feature models over 50, movies and television programs deal with subjects of interest to the older segment of the population, and new products have hit the market. This is a marked contrast to the youth-oriented promotions of the last decade.

Sex is an obvious basis for consumer market analysis. Many of the traditional buying patterns are changing. Men are frequent food shoppers, women are buying gas and arranging for car repair, and both are now concerned with home maintenance and repair. The number of working women has risen considerably in all age groups. In the late 1980s, well over one half of all American women were working outside the home and this trend has continued to grow in the 1990s.

For some products and services, it is useful to analyze the population based on **ethnic origin**. Product preferences, age distribution, population shifts and language will vary. You should be aware of the ethnic breakdown of the geographical area that you are targeting. This data is found in the Census Bureau information dealing with general population characteristics. A business reference librarian can direct you to resources such as the City and County Data Book, which contains statistical information on population distribution.

Family status must be analyzed. During the past decade, two distinct and new groups have emerged: single people living alone and unmarried people living together. Census reports break down family status by number of children and their age ranges, and indicate a rise in the number of single parents.

Education level, **occupation** and **income** are other demographics to be considered. Education level often points to changes in product preference. People with higher levels of education may have more specialized tastes and higher incomes. Occupation is also meaningful. Young executives may earn the same income as auto mechanics, but different attitudes, experiences and other life-style factors of the two groups may lead to different buying patterns. A market requires more than people; it requires money. A knowledge of income, its distribution and how it is spent is essential if you are to know your market.

Over the past years, there has been a tremendous growth in middle- and upper-income markets. This trend is expected to continue. Some of this growth is attributed to dual-income families. Regional income data will help pinpoint your market. Income data on cities will be helpful in choosing your location. Much of this type of information is available through a local chamber of commerce. The trend toward higher income increases the amount of discretionary money available for spending in the marketplace. This usually leads to increased demand for food, clothing, travel and entertainment.

Psychographics

Psychographics are the psychological characteristics of your market and are as important as demographics. The traditional demographic studies gave no insight into why people bought certain products over those of the competition. Marketers began to see the need for analyzing life-style, personal behavior, self-concept and buying style. The study of psychographics and its relationship to marketing is relatively new. It had its beginnings in the early 1950s. At the present time, it is a widely used tool for analyzing the market.

Life-style refers to a person's manner of living. It is a broad category and involves personality characteristics. Life-style relates to a customer's activities, interests, and opinions. It reflects how leisure time is spent. Are evenings spent at home or going out? A study may have identified a market in terms of demographics: a 20 square mile area in which 85 percent of the population is comprised of single or married couples without children who commute more than 30 miles to work. You may assume that this segment of your market would appreciate take-out food, has the money required for its purchase, and looks forward to relaxing with a meal at home after working and commuting. However, psycho-

Life-style: A pattern of living that comprises an individual's activities, interests, and opinions.

graphic studies may show that the majority of that market looks forward to going out to eat.

Personal behavior is tied to personal values. The degree of community involvement, political activity and neighborhood participation reflect the psychological makeup of a person. The degree of cautiousness, skepticism and ambition reflects on buying patterns.

Self-concept refers to how a person sees him- or herself and hopes to be seen by others. The demographics of family size, location, occupation and income level may indicate that an individual would purchase a station wagon, but the psychographics of self-image show that the individual would buy a sports car.

The **buying style** of your market is critical. How often do they make a purchase? Was there a specific reason for the purchase or was it an impulse buy? New products are first purchased by individuals who perceive themselves as adventuresome and open-minded.

Your questionnaire results can form a basis for zeroing in on your customers. They can give you feedback regarding the demographics and psychographics of your study group. Include questions that will generate the information you need.

Putting it Together

The key to market research is gathering useful information: information that is timely and reliable. Market research is an orderly, objective way of learning about the people who will buy your product or use your service. A Target Market Worksheet (pp. 58-59) has been included at the end of this chapter for your use in defining your market. Resources that follow this chapter will help you locate additional sources and gather the data you need.

Remember that marketing is a dynamic process. Customers move, lifestyles change, income levels vary. To work effectively, market research must occur continuously throughout the lifetime of your business. Always be alert for new competition, new products and services, population shifts and new trends.

Because of the current emphasis on fiscal responsibility, on the lowering of the national debt, and on the possibility of higher taxes, the buying public is being much more cautious. A smart business owner will keep up-to-date on demographic and psychographic shifts by studying current census reports, by reading business magazines and trade journals, by listening to news and economic analysts, and by using the powers of observation.

Once you have identified your target market, you are ready to position your business and move into the marketplace. The next section of this book, **Reaching Your Target Market**, will instruct you in the elements involved in contacting your customers and in letting them know that your product or service is available for sale.

Resources
Federal Government
1. Bureau of the Budget

Standard Industrial Classification Manual: This publication lists the SIC numbers issued to major areas of business; for example, the SIC number for piano tuning is #7699. These numbers are the keys to unlocking census data.

Standard Metropolitan Statistical Areas: These publications classify population based upon metropolitan statistical areas rather than city and county boundaries. An MSA is an integrated social and economic unit with a large population nucleus. It centers on one city and includes urban areas.

2. Bureau of the Census
Issues publications covering demographic and economic surveys.

3. Department of Commerce

Census of Business: Retail Area Statistics

Census Tract Manual

City & County Data Book: This book is updated every three years and contains statistical information on population, education, employment, income, housing and retail sales.

County Business Patterns

Directory of Federal Statistics for Local Areas

Facts for Marketers

Measuring Markets: A guide for using federal and state statistical data.

4. Small Business Administration

National Directories for Use in Marketing

Small Marketers Aids: Researching your Market

Statistics and Maps for Market Analysis

State Government

1. State Department of Commerce

2. Office of the Secretary of State

3. State Bookstore

Local Government

1. Regulatory Agencies

2. Urban and Redevelopment Agencies

3. Business License Bureau

Non-Government Sources

1. Banks

2. Chambers of Commerce

3. Community and State Colleges

4. Entrepreneurs (local business owners)

5. Merchant Associations

6. Retired Entrepreneurs (SCORE counselors may be contacted through the SBA)

7. Wholesalers and Suppliers

8. *World Trade Outlook* - provides projections of industrial activity on a global scale

Printed Material

1. Directories that are compiled by Chambers of Commerce and Merchants Associations.

2. Magazines and Journals

   Advertising Age
   Advertising and Sales Promotion
   Business Horizons
   Business Week
   Harvard Business Review
   Industrial Marketing
   Journal of Advertising Research
   Journal of Business
   Journal of Marketing
   Journal of Marketing Research
   Wall Street Journal

3. Phone directory yellow pages

4. Newspapers

Library Resources

Publications and directories available in the business reference section.

1. *Business Periodicals Index*: a monthly listing of business articles appearing in a wide variety of business publications.

2. *Directory of Directories*: describes over 9,000 buyer's guides and directories.

3. *Dun and Bradstreet Directories*: lists companies alphabetically, geographically and by product classification.

4. *Encyclopedia of Associations*: provides information on every major trade and professional association in the United States.

5. *Marketing Information Guide*: provides a monthly annotated bibliography of marketing information.

6. *Standard & Poor's Industry Surveys*: updated statistics and analyses of industries.

7. *Statistical Abstract of the U.S.*: updated annually, provides demographic, economic and social information.

8. *U.S. Industrial Outlook*: provides projections of industrial activity.

Books

Blankenship, A.B., and George Breen, *State of the Art Marketing Research* (Chicago: NTC Business Books, 1993).

Gorton, Keith, and Isoble Doole, *Low Cost Marketing Research: A Guide for Small Business* (New York: Wiley, 1989).

Norman, Jan, *It's Your Business: a Practical Guide to Entrepreneurship* (Santa Ana, CA: Orange County Register, 1993).

Settle, Robert, and Pamela Alreck, *Why They Buy* (New York: John Wiley and Sons, 1989).

Wickham, Penelope (editor), *Demographic Knowhow* (Ithaca, NY: American Demographics Press, 1988).

Target Market Worksheet
Home-Cookin Food Delivery

1. WHO ARE MY CUSTOMERS?

Profile: Results from questionnaires, interviews, mail list results.

Economic level: 52% college graduates
29% professionals
25% management
79% own or are buying homes

Psychological make-up (lifestyle):   - affluent, outgoing   - entertain at home
- value convenience and quick service - conservative

Age range: Average age = 42 years

Sex: Male: 57%
Female: 43%

Income level: Average household income - $58,000
69% income from two wage earners

Buying habits: Do not use coupons.
Quality more important than cost.
Do like to save money.

2. WHERE ARE MY CUSTOMERS LOCATED?

Where do they live: Within city limits of the suburb, Johnson, FL.

Where do they work: 62% commute 20 to 35 miles one way.
24% in Johnson
14% retired

Where do they shop: 32% of commuters shop where they work and arrive home after 6:30 P.M.
Remainder shop in Johnson.

3. PROJECTED SIZE OF THE MARKET: Target group represents 20% of total population within city limits. Total population = 36,000; 20% = 7,200.

Projections indicate that I can prepare and deliver 100 meals per evening, Monday through Friday.

4. WHAT ARE THE CUSTOMERS NEEDS?

a. Convenience and quick service.

b. 32% of commuters shop where they work and arrive home after 6:30 P.M. to avoid congested commute.

c. Value quality - like to save money. Do not use coupons.

d. Want meals in $10 to $15 range.

e.

f.

5. HOW CAN I MEET THOSE NEEDS?

a. Offer FAX number for ordering. Provide weekly menu for order placement.

b. Extend delivery service until 8 P.M. to serve this segment of the market.

c. Stress and use high quality products. Offer discount for repeat business, referrals. i.e.: free pie 5 dinners, 10% discount for standing orders.

d. Price meals at $14 to allow for discounts.

e.

f.

6. WHAT IS UNIQUE ABOUT MY BUSINESS?

Home-cooked meals.
Only delivery service offering full meal: salad, entree, dessert.
Discounts offered to loyal customers.
Extended hours.
FAX service and preprinted menus for ease of ordering.

PART II

Reaching Your Target Market

✔ **Product or Service**

✔ **Place**

✔ **Price**

✔ **Promotion**

✔ **Packaging**

Product or Service

In the first part of this book you identified needs in the marketplace and explored ways in which you could meet those needs. In order to reach the customers you have identified as interested in your product or service, you must now develop a marketing plan. Marketing professionals have long referred to this as the development of a **marketing mix**. This is a combination of factors, often referred to as the "Four Ps," which help you determine the what, where, when, why, and how of your business and of your methods for reaching your customers. What is the product or service, where is it available, when will it be available, why will customers want it, how much does it cost and how will they hear about it?

In the past the "Four Ps" stood for product, place, price and promotion. A fifth "P," packaging, has recently been added. We find that the manner in which a product or service is "packaged" can have a direct bearing on its success in the marketplace.

All of the "Ps" work together in formulating a marketing plan. Therefore, as you work through this section of the book, read all of Part II before taking action. For example, determining a pricing structure (Chapter 9) is dependent upon the production costs you determine in this chapter. Your forms of advertising and promotion (Chapter 10) and their relative costs will also be considered in pricing. Your location and distribution decisions (Chapter 8) may also have an impact on advertising and promotion efforts. This chapter will deal with your product or service and its position in the marketplace.

Marketing mix: The set of product, place, promotion, price and packaging variables that a marketing manager controls and orchestrates to bring a product or service into the marketplace.

Promotion: The communication of information by a seller to influence the attitudes and behavior of potential buyers.

Product or Service Development

Basic to marketing is a clear understanding of your product or service and the unique considerations inherent in their differences. A product is a physical and tangible thing. It can be seen and touched. When you buy it, you own it. What you buy is what you get! A service is a deed provided by one party for another. It is not tangible, it can not be seen or touched, and you do not "own" it. A service is experienced or used. Products are usually produced and then sold. By contrast, services are often sold first and then produced or performed. Products can be produced and stored as inventory; services can't be stored and this can create a challenge in anticipating supply and demand. These differences lead to unique methods of development.

Because products are physical and tangible, they must be produced prior to sale. New product ideas that survived the "researching" stage must now be developed into salable items. During the prototype stage (Chapter 4), you researched acceptable materials, analyzed production methods, found supply sources and looked at customer response and acceptance. Now you will analyze that information and put your results to work.

Let's look at our environmental newsletter example. The results of your marketing research indicated that your customers prefer recycled paper in a natural color, eight pages of text, and readable text in "Schoolbook" type style. Based on these findings, some of your decisions will be:

1. Where can recycled paper be purchased?

2. Is it more cost-effective to purchase the paper directly from the manufacturer or through a printer?

3. What are the costs involved in having an eight page newsletter printed?

4. Is it more cost-effective to purchase a printer and produce the paper in house?

5. What are the costs involved in using a desktop publisher for newsletter development?

6. Is "Schoolbook" type available?

Library references such as *Thomas Register of American Manufacturers* help you identify and locate manufacturers and are an excellent resource for locating sources of supply. Yellow page directories can point the way to local paper suppliers, print shops and desktop publishers. When you have located sources of supply for all of the elements involved in the production of your product, have determined that those sources can produce in the quantity and in the time frame required, and have found the best pricing structures, you will be ready to begin production of your product.

Although service performance differs from product creation, the marketer must look at some of the same considerations. In the example of the home delivery of foods, the target market may have indicated that it prefers biodegradable cardboard containers, wants meals delivered within one-half hour of order placement, and prefers a variety of foreign foods. Based on these findings, you will need to decide on answers to the following questions:

1. Where can biodegradable food containers be purchased in bulk and what are their cost?

2. Can foods be kept hot in the desired containers and within the customers' preferred time frame?

3. Where can the specialty foods and seasonings be purchased and what are their costs?

Just as with product development, the reference section of the library, the yellow page section of the phone book, the local chamber of commerce and the Small Business Administration will be able to direct you to the information you need.

It is not enough to just deal with the physical production of the product or the single provision of a service. To market effectively, we must think about the "whole" product or service provided and make sure that all of the needs of the target market are being met. Sometimes a single product isn't enough to meet the needs of customers. An assortment of different products, an array of services, or a combination of product and service may be required. For example, a company offering kayak lessons and trips (service) may find that its target market would like to purchase clothing and other gear for kayaking and books on the subject (products.) The restaurant promoting "home-cooked dinners" (product) may find the need for home delivery (service). Whether you provide a product, a service or a blend of both, providing what the customer wants and needs is an ongoing challenge.

In order to reach your market in an effective manner, you may have to provide a **product or service line**. This refers to a set of individual prod-

Products: Anything capable of satisfying needs, including tangible items, services, and ideas.

ucts or services that are closely related by being produced or provided in a similar manner, sold to the same target market, made available through the same outlets and/or priced within the same range. For example, a desktop publisher may format and produce books, newsletters, brochures and other promotional items. A clock repair shop may find the need to expand into providing watch and music box repair. An **individual product or service** is a particular item within a line.

Business owners generally think in terms of developing an individual product or service when starting a new business or expanding an existing one. You may have more success in reaching your customers by also providing related products or services. It is important to listen to your target market or customers. Find out what products or services they want and develop a product or service line to meet their needs.

Positioning

Throughout your marketing experience, you will hear the term positioning. A product or service position is determined by its image projected in terms of the competition, pricing, packaging, distribution, location and timing of market entry.

For some products, the best position is directly against the competition. This is evidenced when companies such as Pepsi-Cola® and Coca-Cola® develop new product lines. Both companies have a similar product line appealing to the same market. If the competition is established and has a strong market presence, you may want to use your position to establish uniqueness. A few years ago Hertz® was well established in the car rental business. Avis® capitalized on being number two and trying harder.

Some stores are known for high quality merchandise and higher prices. Others have the image of discount stores. Once your position is established, it is very difficult to change that position in terms of price and quality. Discount stores have a hard time upgrading their image through the introduction of higher quality merchandise at higher prices. By the same token, the introduction of discount products into a high-scale store would have a negative reaction. The move would cloud the company's image, confuse the customers and probably reduce the store's share of the target market.

Distribution channels: All of the individuals and organizations involved in the process of moving products from producer to consumer.

Your market research will have given you insights into the ways in which to position your product or service. You know your competition, how they advertise and who they serve. You have compared the pricing structures, the distribution channels, the packaging, and the locations of competitors. Positioning is much like a ranking system. Determine where you want to be on the ladder. Choose the most effective combination of products and/or services to offer as a product line based upon feedback from your customers. Determine where you want your product line to be positioned in the marketplace. The next chapters will give you information on methods of distribution, location choices, pricing structures, timing of market entry, promotion and packaging as you get ready to enter the marketplace.

Summary

While developing your product or service and determining its position, it is essential that you keep the needs and preferences of your customers in mind. Your market research has provided you with information on what is acceptable to your customers in terms of product "look" and packaging. You have determined that your market wants their "home-cooked" meals delivered in microwave-proof cartons for reheating. Your newsletter readers prefer an eight page publication. While researching sources of supply, you may discover that cardboard containers are less costly and that a newsletter printed in a smaller type on four pages is cheaper. Don't lose sight of the needs of your consumers. If their expected needs aren't met, you will lose their interest in purchasing your product or using your service.

Resources

Books

Bangs, David H., Jr., *Creating Customers* (Chicago: Upstart Publishing Co., 1992).

Bangs, David H., Jr., *The Market Planning Guide, 4th edition* (Chicago: Upstart Publishing Co., 1995).

Bobrow, Edwin E., *Pioneering New Products: A Market Survival Guide* (Homewood, IL: Dow Jones-Irwin, 1987).

Burstiner, Irving, *The Small Business Handbook* (New York: Prentice Hall Press, 1989).

Franklin, Reece, *Inventor's Marketing Handbook* (Chino Hills, CA: AAJA Publishing Company, 1989).

Hall, Stephen, *From Kitchen to Market* (Chicago: Upstart Publishing Co., 1992).

King, Tony, *How to Invent Your Way to Wealth* (Wilmington, CA: Knolls West Press, 1989).

Linneman, Robert E. and John Stanton, *Making Niche Marketing Work*, (New York: McGraw Hill, 1992).

Mosley, Thomas, *Marketing Your Invention* (Chicago: Upstart Publishing Co., 1992).

Reynolds, Don, *Crackerjack Positioning* (Rogue River, OR: Atwood Publishing, 1993).

References

Assael, Henry, *Marketing: Principles & Strategy* (Orlando, FL: Holt, Rinehart, and Winston, 1990). **

McCarthy, E. Jerome, and William Perreault, *Basic Marketing* (Homewood, IL: Irwin Publishing, 1987). **

**College textbooks that contain good sections on product development.

Thomas Register of American Manufacturers (New York: Thomas Publishing Company, annual).

Agencies

Consumer Products Safety Commission
Bureau of Compliance
5401 Westbard Avenue
Bethesda, MD 20207
1(800) 638-2772 (Recorded message tape)

Request information and booklets on laws and regulations regarding product design:

The Federal Hazardous Substances Act
Consumer Product Safety Act of 1972
The Flammable Fabrics Act

U.S. Department of Commerce
Office of Consumer Affairs
Washington, DC 20233

Request booklets such as:

Consumer Product Safety

Federal Trade Commission
Office of Consumer Affairs
Washington, DC 20233

Request trade practice rules that apply to your business or product line.

Food and Drug Administration
5600 Fishers Lane
Rockville, MD 20857

Contact on a federal, state and local level to determine requirements governing food-related products.

National Institute of Standards & Technology
U.S. Department of Commerce
Gaithersburg, MD 20899

Write for information on special labeling required for products containing precious metals.

U.S. Small Business Administration
P.O. Box 46521
Denver, CO 80201
(800) 827-5722 (SBA Small Business Answer Desk)

Inventory Management MP22...$ .50
Buying for Retail Stores MP18...$1.00

Superintendent of Documents
P.O. Box 371954
Pittsburgh, PA 15250-7954
(202) 783-3238

Request listing of publications such as:

Decision Points in Developing New Products
Inventory Management - Manufacturing/Service

U.S. Fish & Wildlife Service
Division of Law Enforcement
Department of the Interior
Washington, DC 20240

Write for guidelines and restrictions if you work with feathers, bones or endangered species.

FWS 069 - *Federal Laws Restricting Commerce in Wildlife*

Place

The second "P" in the marketing mix equation stands for **place**. It refers to the decisions a company makes to insure that a product or service gets to the customer at the right location and in the right manner. We will expand place to include methods of distribution as well as your business location. The ways in which you get your raw materials and products and the means of getting your product or service to the customer are also marketing decisions.

Methods of Distribution

Distribution is a major component of the marketing mix. The distribution process has been compared to a pipeline or channel. Information, orders, products, services and payments flow from consumer to product manufacturer or service provider and back again. In order to work smoothly, these entities must cooperate and have a full understanding of each other's responsibilities.

Product

If you are a manufacturer of a product, you may wish to develop a flow chart in order to examine the channels available for distribution of your goods. The following are examples of product distribution channels:

1. Direct sales to customers

2. Sales through mail order

3. Sales through a retail outlet

4. Sales through a manufacturer's representative

5. Delivery directly to customers

6. Delivery to retail outlets

7. Sales and delivery through wholesalers

8. Delivery by drop shipment

As you can see, distribution involves sales and delivery. In marketing, you must analyze how an order is placed and how a product is delivered. For example, an order for take-out food will be placed over the phone. Delivery of the food will require a delivery van and driver. In the card game example we have used in this book, orders may come directly from consumers, from retail outlets or through manufacturers' reps. If you sell directly to the customer or to a retail outlet, you will be responsible for order fulfillment and shipping. If you sell through a manufacturer's representative, you may ship to a warehouse for consolidation of your order with others. It is important to look at all of the costs involved in your sales and delivery systems in order to choose the most cost-effective channels. This information will also be important when you determine a selling price for your product or service in Chapter 9.

Direct sales: The process whereby the producer sells to the user, ultimate consumer or retailer without intervening middlemen.

Direct sales to the consumer can be made through door-to-door representation, through display booths at events such as fairs, trade shows and mall events or through mail or phone order. You will solicit the order on a one-on-one basis. This method allows the business owner or a company representative to meet and communicate with the consumer and to gather information useful to future marketing. Delivery can be made at the time of sale, or later by personal delivery or shipment by common carrier.

Mail order selling is a unique way of doing business. Orders are generated through the mail with catalogs, brochures, telephone solicitations and other advertising methods. The customer sends the order and payment through the mail; the product is returned to the customer through the mail or other shipping method.

Catalogs are currently a popular marketing tool. We see specialty catalogs for sale at chain bookstores. Home television shopping shows find merchandise through catalogs. You may choose to develop your own or be included in an established catalog. Review catalogs and see if your product would be appropriate for addition to their current product line. You may be asked to pay a fee for being included or you may pay a percentage of sales. If your market analysis indicates that your customers purchase by mail, contact the catalog company regarding sale of your item through its catalog. Catalog companies may submit a purchase order and you will ship merchandise directly to them. Or the company may submit copies of customer purchase orders and ask that you **drop ship** the merchandise. In the first case, you are responsible for delivering the products to the catalog company. In the second case, you are responsible for filling and shipping individual orders. If you are involved in drop shipment of goods, clarify who is responsible for collection of sales tax and shipping charges.

The marketer involved in mail order must be aware of the postal regulations that affect mail order, the different tax laws in each state into which mail is delivered, and the Federal Trade Commission rules. For example, the FTC requires that delivery on all mail order be made within 30 days. If you will be using mail order, contact the FTC and the Interstate Commerce Commission for shipping rules. Their addresses are listed in the Resource section following this chapter.

Resellers are the wholesalers and the retailers. They are the people we call the "middlemen." They operate between you as the product supplier and the customer. If you sell your product through a **retail store,** you may represent yourself and sell directly to the retail outlet for a wholesale price plus shipping and handling. The store will submit a "purchase order" through the mail or by phone. You will fill that order by direct delivery or common carrier shipment.

Middleman: A person or company who performs functions or renders services involved in the purchase and/or sale of goods in their flow from producer to consumer.

Some stores will take products on **consignment**. This is the typical selling arrangement in the art and craft field. The consignment arrangement provides a good way for the product producer and a store owner to introduce a new product and to test market a price. However, there are some disadvantages to this method of selling.

The retail outlet agrees to display the item for sale but is not responsible for theft or damage. Payment is made after an item is sold. You may find your inventory tied up for long periods of time, which could lead to cash flow problems.

The shop owners have a vested interest in selling the merchandise for which they have already paid. You may find that your products are not as aggressively marketed as the products that are "owned" by the seller.

Consigned goods remain the property of the seller (manufacturer) until they are sold to the customer by the retail store. However, if the shop should file for bankruptcy, your goods may be seized and be subject to the claims of creditors. The law regarding consignment differs by state.

Contact your state legislature in order to determine the degree of protection in your state.

Because of the risks involved, this may not be a desirable alternative for you. However, if consignment is the normal method of sale for your product, limit your risks. Research the reputation of the store by contacting other individuals who have dealt with it on a consignment basis. Limit the number of items you offer on consignment. Require a consignment agreement. Visit the store often and follow up on the manner in which your merchandise is promoted, displayed and maintained.

Sales representative: An independent salesperson who directs effort to selling your products or service to others but is not an employee of your company.

You may choose to market through a **manufacturer's** or **sales representative**. A manufacturer's rep will handle your product and represent it to the retailer through trade show exposure or direct sales contact. Sales reps usually carry a line of related but non-competitive products. They cover specific territories. Reps usually work strictly on commission and receive a percentage of the wholesale price. You must furnish the sales materials: price lists, brochures, sample sets. You must have a written contract specifying the territory, terms of sale, allowance for returned merchandise, commission percentage and terms of contract.

Commission: A percentage of the principal or of the income that an agent receives as compensation for services.

Manufacturers' reps can be important members of your marketing team. They are an excellent source of information regarding trends in your field because their ideas are based on the demands they observe in the marketplace. Let the rep know when you have a new product or design. Trade journals and directories of manufacturers' representatives will give you listings of resellers covering your field and are available in the library.

Wholesaling: Businesses and individuals engaged in the activity of selling products to retailers, organizational users or other wholesalers.

Wholesalers serve as a distributive link between the producer and the retailer or user. They purchase goods from manufacturers for their own account and resell those goods to other businesses such as retailers, other manufacturers or end users. Wholesalers are also called distributors or jobbers. They carry stock in large amounts and redistribute it in small quantities. For example, the manufacturer of the card game wants to sell the new product in stores across the nation. Rather than contacting individual retailers and delivering each order, the manufacturer can locate a few distributors who have branches or access to those retailers. The costs of individual delivery, contact of retailers, storage and handling can be reduced. Since manufacturers are concerned with the need to have their products carried by those retail stores in which consumers expect to find such items, the broad market coverage manufacturers' need can be provided by a wholesaler.

Wholesalers offer additional services as well. Some extend credit, offer advice on store locations and give information on how to package and display goods. Many provide promotional materials and notify customers of new products coming into the market.

The most important function of a wholesaler-distributor is inventory control. Inventory control is working within the practical limits of space, money, personnel and time. When a customer places an order, it is expected to be filled in a short time. The entire wholesale operation revolves around serving customers economically, efficiently and effectively. It is important to work closely with your wholesaler and to keep the lines of communication open.

Inventory: A list of assets being held for sale.

Wholesalers generally are paid a percentage of sales, offer co-op promotional opportunities for a fee and maintain an allowance against returns account. Payment schedules may vary. Review all contracts to determine when you will be paid and who will pay shipping charges.

Just-in-time (JIT) distribution means producing exactly what is required by the market just in time to be delivered to customers. This system was developed by the Japanese as a production control method rather than a distribution system. The idea was to get materials to the production line as they were needed in order to reduce inventory costs. The concept was extended to distribution in the 1980s when high interest rates and high taxes increased the costs of inventory. By eliminating inventory, overhead costs were reduced.

Overhead: A general term for costs of materials and services not directly adding to or readily identifiable with the product or service being sold.

The process requires that goods be produced on an as-ordered basis. A customer places an order, raw materials are ordered, the product is manufactured and that product is delivered to the customer. Transportation is a key component since such a system requires more frequent delivery of smaller quantities. Because of cost, selection of delivery method is one of the important decisions in this system. It is important that the increased transportation costs are offset by the decreased inventory and storage costs.

The delivery part of distribution involves working with the four major forms of transportation: railroads, trucks, ships and airplanes. You must decide on the form of transportation to use and the particular carriers. Your goal is to move the right goods to the right place at the right time for the right cost. Physical distribution costs are a substantial part of the operating costs in many companies. Each form of transportation is suited to a particular need. There are weight and size limitations for some carriers. What are the shipping trends for your industry? How are goods shipped by the competition? Contact the Interstate Commerce Commission regarding guidelines and restrictions on your products. The U.S. Postal Service can give you information regarding mail delivery. The yellow page section of your phone directory will list common carriers in your area.

Service

Unlike products that are produced, sold and then used, services are often sold first, then produced and used at the same time. Simultaneous production and use creates unique considerations regarding sales and delivery. The following are examples of service distribution channels:

1. Service performed at customer's location

2. Service performed at business location

3. Service performed through communication link

4. Combination of the above

Services performed at a customer's location require the use of business transportation in the form of a delivery van, repair truck or other vehicle. The cost of these vehicles as well as the salaries of the repair person must be considered in determining the hourly rate you will charge for your service.

The service may be performed at the business location. The customer comes to your shop with an item needing repair: a tooth to be filled, a lamp to be rewired, clothing to be cleaned.

An example of a service performed through a communication link would be airline reservations made by phone, with the tickets being delivered by Federal Express or the postal service.

Combinations of the above occur when a watch to be repaired is mailed to the repair shop and later picked up by the customer. A manuscript can be transmitted via computer modem to a desktop publisher for editing and final formatting before printing. With advances in electronic and computer technology, most service businesses will use a combination of delivery systems in order to reach their customers.

Choose sales and delivery methods based upon what is acceptable to your target market. How do they expect to order and to receive your product or service? Consider all of the costs involved in the methods you will use. When starting out with a new idea and a new business, you may find it more cost-effective to operate on a "do-it-yourself" basis. You may wish to deal directly with retailers and customers and provide your own warehousing in a small, self-storage location. You may wish to provide your service in the customer's home or through a shop set up as a home-based business. Your decision will also take into account your market, your image, your cash flow and your location.

Location

Among the general factors to be considered when deciding on a business location are accessibility to the market, location of the competition, sources of supplies, availability of a labor force, means of transportation and square-footage cost. Other considerations are zoning regulations, area crime rates and neighborhood image.

Your most important consideration in choosing a location is your ability to satisfy your target market. Your customers must be able to reach your business easily, safely and pleasantly.

One of the most effective ways to evaluate location is to do a "map analysis." Draw a map of the area in which you wish to locate. Have a copy shop run off some duplicates and one transparency. On the transparency, indicate the location sites available within your target area and mark them with a colored pen or assign each of them a number. You will be coding information onto the duplicate maps. You will be able to place the transparency over the coded map in order to get a feeling for each site. For instance, take one of the duplicate maps to the police department. Ask about area crime rates. Shade the high-crime area on your map. When you place the transparency over the shaded duplicate, you will be able to see if any of your potential locations fall within that area.

Market

On another duplicate map, shade in the areas in which your target market lives, shops or works. Again use the transparency overlay and see if your customers will be able to reach you easily. Is there freeway access, good traffic flow and adequate parking? Customers are concerned about safety. Can they reach your place of business with a feeling of security? Your crime rate map will show if they have to pass through any high-crime areas on the way to your establishment. Customers' trips to your business should be pleasant. Drive and walk the routes your customers will have to take. Get a feeling for the neighborhood. A **Location Analysis Worksheet** (see pp. 82-83) has been provided for your use at the end of this chapter. Fill one out and use it in conjunction with your area maps for a thorough site evaluation.

Supplies

If you are in a retail or service business, can suppliers reach you easily? Are there one-way streets and confusing traffic patterns? If you are a manufacturer, locate your sources of supply. Would it be more cost-effective to locate near your raw materials?

Labor Force

Another location consideration is the availability of employees. Some areas do not have an adequate group of people to form a labor pool. The prevailing wage rate in the area may be out of line with competitors' rates in other areas. The local chamber of commerce will be able to give you wage and labor statistics for the location you are considering.

Competition

How many similar businesses are located nearby? What does their sales volume appear to be? Use one of your maps to illustrate the location of your competition.

Cost

Office space for minimal rent is not always the best. There usually is a reason why the rent is low. Find out why the space is available, how long it has been vacant and the history of the previous tenants. If there has been a frequent turnover in occupancy, it may be considered a "bad location." The chamber of commerce can give you information on average square-footage costs for your area. Check with the local zoning commission regarding any rezoning planned for the surrounding area. Take a walk around the area. Does the location project the image you have for your business?

Home-Based Business

There are advantages to locating your business in your home. A home-based business may be a practical solution for the parent with child care concerns. If you are not making on-site sales and conduct most of your business off-site, you can save overhead costs with an office in your home. Some other considerations in a home-based business are distances to suppliers and customers, locations of competitors, future business goals, type of neighborhood, insurance requirements and zoning regulations. Zoning laws vary with each city and are mainly concerned with the potential for increased traffic flow, noise pollution and change of the character of the neighborhood. The Internal Revenue Service and your local Zoning Commission and Business License Bureau will be able to provide information and guidelines for this location choice.

Shopping Centers

You may consider locating in a shopping center. These sites are pre-planned as merchandising units. On-site parking is available. Customers can drive in, park and shop easily and quickly. You can take advantage of customers drawn to the area by other stores.

There may be some limitations, however. You will be a part of a merchant team. You will be expected to pay your share of the site budget, which may include items such as co-op advertising and promotional activities and building, landscaping and parking lot maintenance. You may have to keep regular store hours, maintain your windows and premises in a pre-scribed manner and conform to established display guidelines.

Business Incubators

A new entity has emerged in the location market: the business incubator facility. To reduce overhead costs for new businesses, the incubator pro-gram offers a number of services to tenants through a centralized resource station. Usually included in the tenant package are reception and tele-phone answering, maintenance of the building and grounds, conference room facilities, and shipping and receiving services. Other services may include complete clerical services at a nominal charge. Incubator facili-ties are targeted toward small start-up and new firms. Square-footage costs are low. The new businesses are expected to remain for two to three years. At that point it is hoped they will be successful enough to relocate.

Enterprise Zones

We have been hearing a great deal about the advantages of locating in enterprise zones as communities work toward redeveloping depressed areas. Companies locating in these zones can take advantage of signifi-cant tax incentives and marketing programs. Enterprise zone communi-ties are committed to attracting new business investment and offer such incentives as reduction or elimination of local permit and construction-related fees and faster processing of plans and permits. Information on enterprise zones in your area can be obtained through the Department of Commerce, the SBA and the local Chamber of Commerce.

Evaluate the possibilities of the home-based business, the shopping cen-ter location, the business incubator and the enterprise zone site in terms of your business. Carefully analyze all of the factors we have discussed in this chapter. The location of your business can well mean the differ-ence between success and failure.

Summary

Obviously, the needs, attitudes, and location of your target market must be considered when making distribution and location choices. Where do they expect to purchase your product? How will they make use of your service? Will they find a home-based location acceptable?

Don't overlook the needs of your suppliers and your employees. Are they located within a convenient radius of your business? Will your suppliers be able to deliver to a home-based location and does your home-office license allow you to have employees?

Take time during the development stage of your business to look at all of the ramifications of your location and distribution decisions. Good working relationships with distributors, sales representatives, landlords and other "partners" take time to develop. Location and distribution decisions are harder to change once established.

Resources

Books

Blanchard, B., *Logistics Engineering and Management* (Englewood Cliffs, NJ: Prentice-Hall, 1986).

Bly, Robert, *Selling Your Services* (New York: Henry Holt, 1991).

Davidson, Jeffrey, *Marketing for the Home-Based Business* (Hollbrook, MA: Bob Adams Inc., 1990).

Pinson, Linda, and Jerry Jinnett, *The Home-Based Entrepreneur* (Chicago: Upstart Publishing Co., 1993).

References

Chilton's Distribution Magazine (Periodical)
Thomas Foster, Editor
Chilton Way
Radnor, PA 19089
(215) 964-4379

How-to information on inventory control, transportation and business logistics.

Direct Marketing Market Place
Comprehensive directory about leading companies that sell by mail. Information includes service and supply sources.

Directory of Manufacturer's Sales Agents
Directory of sales agencies representing manufacturers. Agencies are arranged alphabetically, by state and by product classification.

Agencies

Council of Logistics Management
2803 Butterfield Road, Suite 380
Oak Brook, IL 60521
(708) 574-0985

Offers information on management and coordination of transportation warehousing and handling of goods.

Federal Trade Commission
Pennsylvania Avenue & 6th Street NW
Washington, DC 20580
(202) 326-2000

Incubators for Small Business
Office of Private Sector Initiatives, SBA
1441 L Street NW, Room 317
Washington, DC 20416

Interstate Commerce Commission
12th Street and Constitution Avenue, NW
Washington, DC 20015

Manufacturers' Agents National Association
23016 Mill Creek Road
Laguna Hills, CA 92654
(714)859-4040

National Association of Wholesalers-Distributors
1725 K Street, NW
Washington, DC 20006
(202)872-0885

U.S. Department of Transportation Library
Room 2200, M-493.3
400 7th Street SW
Washington, DC 20590
(202) 366-0746

The department's library will try to answer your questions related to transportation.

U.S. Small Business Administration
P.O. Box 46521
Denver, CO 80201
(800) 827-5722 (SBA Small Business Answer Desk)

Locating or Relocating your Business MP2...$1.00
Choosing a Retail Location MP10...$1.00
Selling by Mail Order MT9...$1.00
Is the Independent Sales Agent for You? MT3...$ .50
Business Plan for Small Service Firms MP11...$1.00

Location Analysis Worksheet

1. ADDRESS: 271 Adams Street
            Blair, NY 07682

2. NAME, ADDRESS, PHONE NUMBER OF REALTOR/CONTACT PERSON:
            James Johnson
            Century Realty   621-7093
            622 Mason Street
            Blair, NY 07682

3. SQUARE FOOTAGE/COST:
   Retail shop space of 1000 square feet @$2.00/sq. ft.
   30 feet of window display area fronting on high foot traffic area.
   Classroom area in back of store.

4. HISTORY OF LOCATION:
   Previous occupant—retail clothing outlet occupied.
   Occupied site for 7 years. Moved to bigger store.
   Vacant 2 months.

5. LOCATION IN RELATION TO TARGET MARKET:
   Primary retail and business sector for Blair.
   Draws customers from 20 mile radius.

6. TRAFFIC PATTERNS FOR CUSTOMERS:
   Bus stop - 1/2 block.
   Easy access from First Avenue and Main Street
   Traffic lights at crosswalks.

7. TRAFFIC PATTERNS FOR SUPPLIERS:
   Alley access for deliveries.

8. AVAILABILITY OF PARKING (include diagram):
   Diagonal parking - 12 spaces in front of store.
   Parking lot one block away.

9. CRIME RATE FOR THE AREA:
   24-hour security in business sector.
   Active neighborhood watch in surrounding residential area.

10. QUALITY OF PUBLIC SERVICES (e.g., police, fire protection):
   Police station - 6 blocks
   Fire station - 2 miles
   Fire alarm, sprinkler system, smoke alarms in place.

11. NOTES OF WALKING TOUR OF THE AREA:
     Homes well tended on north side.
     Apartment house 2 blocks south - 2 abandoned cars.
     Debris piled in vacant lot - 3 blocks east.

12. NEIGHBORING SHOPS AND LOCAL BUSINESS CLIMATE:
     Dry cleaning/shoe repair
     Restaurant
     Good foot traffic. Association of Business Owners oversees the area.

13. ZONING REGULATIONS:
     Commercial

14. ADEQUACY OF UTILITIES (get information from utility company representatives):
     6 phone lines into site.
     2 bathrooms in shop.
     City water, sewer. 220 wiring in place. No gas available.

15. AVAILABILITY OF RAW MATERIALS/SUPPLIES:
     UPS daily delivery

16. AVAILABILITY OF LABOR FORCE:
     Temporary agency in business center.
     University 5 miles away.
     High school 8 miles away.

17. LABOR RATE OF PAY FOR THE AREA:
     $5.50/hour average for store salespeople.
     $10.00/hour for store manager.

18. HOUSING AVAILABILITY FOR EMPLOYEES:
     Apartment and single-family homes available in 10 mile radius.
     Average rental for 2 bedroom = $450
     Average sale 2 bedroom = $86,000

19. TAX RATES (state, county, income, payroll, special assessments):
     State income = 7%
     State sales tax = 6.5%

20. EVALUATION OF SITE IN RELATION TO COMPETITION:
Smith Sporting Goods—6 miles away—has better parking, located closer to university and high school.
This location is housed in a mini mall and offers more products and services, has a lower square footage cost, and has more foot traffic than the location of Smith Sporting Goods.

Price

Pricing is also a marketing decision, combining market research with financial analysis. To be successful, a business owner must establish prices for goods and services that will allow for a profit margin, will be competitive with similar businesses, and will be acceptable to the customer. Pricing can "make or break" a business. If the price is wrong, it won't matter that everything else is right.

Price: The exchange of value of a product or service from the perspective of both the buyer and the seller.

Finding the Price Ceiling and Price Floor

One of the problems we have as business owners is that we price a product or service at what we **want** it to sell for, rather than at what it **will** sell for. There are two important factors to keep in mind when developing a pricing structure.

1. **Price ceiling**: First recognize that the market determines the price at which a product or service will sell, not your costs. You will need to determine the price ceiling, or the top price, a customer will pay for your product or service. Market research will help you arrive at that figure. Your questionnaires and interview feedback will show what a customer will expect to pay. The information from trade and professional organizations will indicate pricing trends and guidelines. Evaluation of the pricing structure of your competition will indicate what the market is currently paying. The principle to remember is that products or services are bought on the basis of perceived value in the minds of buyers, not on the basis of what it costs you to produce or purchase a product or to provide a service.

Price ceiling: The highest amount that a customer will pay for a product or a service based upon perceived value.

85

Price floor: The lowest amount a business owner can charge for a product or service and still meet all expenses.

2. **Price floor**: Even though the cost of your product or service is not directly related to what the customer is willing to pay for it, costs are of extreme importance to you as the business owner. You must be aware of how much it costs you to produce your product or provide your service. This means that you must take into account all of the operating and other expenses of the business. You must also know your desired annual net profit. How much do you need to make to feel that your business has been profitable? Evaluation of your costs and your desired profits allows you to establish a price floor, the price below which you cannot sell and make the necessary profit.

Successful businesses operate between their price floor and price ceiling. This margin allows for returns, damage, sales and discounts.

As previously stated, the price ceiling is established through market research. The price floor is determined by financial analysis. There are four major elements to consider in setting a price for a product or service:

1. How much does it cost to produce the product or to provide the service? (analyze cost of goods to be sold)

2. What are all of the costs involved in operating the business? (determine variable and fixed expenses)

3. How much profit do you want to make? (personal decision)

4. Will the customer buy your product or service at the price that you have set? (market research)

Financial Analysis

Profit margin: The difference between your selling price and all of your costs.

The most common error in determining the cost of a product or service is the failure to account for **all** of the costs that are involved in producing a product or in providing a service, and in the general operation of a business. Most business owners mistakenly think that costing involves only those expenses related directly to the product or service; if a product's wholesale cost is $4 and the retail price is $12, a gross profit of $8 is realized. On the surface this looks like a good profit margin. However, we have not accounted for shipping expense, office overhead, vehicle costs, commissions and salaries, advertising and rent. These are also costs of running the business and must be paid for from the gross profits. Determining the cost of a product or service means looking at all of the expenses involved in running your business.

If you are selling a product, you must calculate what is called the **cost of goods to be sold** (inventory). This will be the wholesale purchase price of a finished product or the cost of materials plus labor for manufacturing the product. If you are a retailer, an important aspect in determining the selling price of the product is the wholesale price of that product or what it costs you for its purchase. A business that provides a service generally will not have to consider the cost of goods to be sold.

Cost of goods sold: The direct cost to the business owner of those items that will be sold to customers. The cost of raw materials plus the cost of labor in the production of a product.

You must also determine the **variable** expenses involved. These are the costs directly related to your product or service. For example, advertising, delivery vehicle expenses, freight and sales commissions will be in this category. They are volume related: as the volume of sales increases, these costs will increase; as sales go down, these costs will decrease. These costs may also be called "selling" or "direct" expenses because they are directly related to your product or service and they will vary depending upon volume of business.

Fixed expenses refer to costs not directly related to your production or rendering of services. They are the types of expenses that all businesses have in common. For example, licenses, office supplies, office salaries, maintenance, rents, utilities and professional fees are a few of the costs which are not related to volume of business. They must be paid each month even if no sales occur. These costs may also be called "administrative" or "indirect" expenses.

What is the **desired annual net income** that you want to generate from your business activity? Project the amount of money you would like to pocket after all costs and expenses are paid. We can be misled by the "gross profit," which is merely the total sales revenue minus the cost of goods sold and indicates volume of business. The true test of a business's viability is its "net profit" or the bottom line amount remaining after all the expenses and taxes have been paid. This is what the business owner "earns."

Revenue: Total sales during a stated period.

At the end of this chapter we have provided a worksheet for determining total annual expenses and a Cash to be Paid Out Worksheet (p. 92) to help you realize and record all of the expenses which may be incurred by your business.

Hourly Rate Formula

The **Hourly Rate Formula** covers the means of arriving at an hourly rate to charge in a service industry. To complete the formula you will need to determine your desired annual net income. How much profit would you like to have at the end of the year? Also figure out how many **billable** hours you will work per year on the service you will provide. Remember that the hours spent on office work, errand running and other miscellaneous business-related work, while necessary, do not generate income. For this formula, project the number of hours that will generate income. Also determine your annual expenses, which should be on your Cash to be Paid Out Worksheet.

To compute the Hourly Rate, use the following formula. Add the **desired annual net income** to the **total annual expenses** and divide by the **number of billable hours worked per year**. This formula will give you the hourly rate you must charge in order to realize your desired net income. Refer to the sample Hourly Rate Formula Worksheet (see p. 91) at the end of this chapter. The following data has been used to compute the rate:

> Desired annual net income = $45,000
> Total annual expenses = $37,000
> (From Cash to be Paid Out Worksheet)
> Number of billable hours worked per year = 1,000
> (20 hours per week x 50 weeks)

According to the formula, in order to net $45,000 per year with annual expenses of $37,000, you will have to work 1000 hours per year and charge $82 per hour. Perhaps your market research has indicated that your customers do not expect to pay over $75 per hour and that the average hourly rate charged by your competition is $72 per hour. Strict adherence to the above figures will place you out of the market; your price ceiling is too high. In order to make your business viable, you will have to lower the hourly rate.

This formula allows for flexibility. Refer to the example (on p. 91) at the end of this chapter for an illustration. A decrease in your annual expenses will decrease the rate per hour that you must receive. Lower your annual net income, lower your annual expenses or work more hours.

Perhaps you can make more profit by working more billable hours per year. If you do this, be sure to increase your annual expenses accordingly. If you work more hours, you will be increasing the use of utilities, consumable supplies, etc.

Formula for Manufacturers

The **formula for manufacturers** will help you determine a wholesale value for your product. You will need to compute the cost of your labor.

Figure the amount of time needed to make one item and the hourly wage to be paid for its production. Be realistic! Even though you may begin your business by manufacturing your products, success in the marketplace will dictate that you increase production and hire workers accordingly. What would you pay an employee to complete one item? Now determine the cost of materials for making one unit. Figure how many units one person could produce per year. Estimate your annual expenses and your desired annual profit.

The formula for determining the **price per unit** is as follows: Determine the manufacturing cost by multiplying the **number of units to be produced in one year** by the **cost of labor and material for one unit**. Second, add the **manufacturing cost total** to the **estimated annual expenses** and the **desired annual profit**. This total is then divided by the **number of units to be produced during the year**. This will give you the wholesale price you must charge to reach your desired annual income. Refer to the sample Formula for Manufacturers Worksheet (p. 94) at the end of this chapter. The following data has been used to compute the rate:

Cost of labor per item = $2.50
(Compute the amount of time needed to make one item. In the example, one half-hour is used. Figure the hourly wage. In this case, $5.00. The cost of labor per item would be $2.50).

Cost of materials for one unit = $2.50
Estimated annual expenses = $93,250
Desired annual profit = $50,000
Number of units produced per year = 10,000

If you are manufacturing an item to be sold in retail stores, be aware that most stores will **keystone,** or double the wholesale price, to arrive at a retail price. Since your wholesale price is $19.33, you can assume a retail price of $38.66. Perhaps this is too high for the consumer. Again, your market research will have determined the price ceiling or the top price your customers will expect to pay for the item you are offering. You may want to consider adjusting some of the figures you are using. Examples of the flexibility of this formula are shown on the sample form (p. 94) at the end of this chapter.

These formulas and examples are offered as guides in helping you determine your wholesale product price and hourly service rate. They are only as accurate as the figures being used. The only significant profit is net profit after taxes. It is a common misconception that "the more you sell, the more you will make." Profits are tied directly to both sales and costs. Any change in either will affect the profit. Increased sales can lead to increased profits as long as costs are kept under control. The best possible situation would be to increase sales while decreasing costs. This is the goal of every entrepreneur.

Resources

Books

Bangs, David, *The Cash Flow Control Guide* (Chicago: Upstart Publishing Co., 1992).

Pinson, Linda, and Jerry Jinnett, *Keeping the Books, 2nd edition,* (Chicago: Upstart Publishing Co. 1996).

References

Assael, Henry, *Marketing: Principles & Strategy* (Orlando, FL: Holt, Rinehart, and Winston, 1990). **

McCarthy, E. Jerome, and William Perreault, *Basic Marketing* (Homewood, IL: Irwin Publishing, 1987). **

**College textbooks that contain good sections on pricing strategies.

Agencies

U.S. Small Business Administration
P.O. Box 46521
Denver, CO 80201
(800) 827-5722 (SBA Small Business Answer Desk)

Profit Costing and Pricing for Manufacturers FM2...$1.00
Understanding Cash Flow FM4...$1.00
Pricing Checklist for Small Retailers FM12...$1.00
Pricing your Products and Services Profitably FM13...$1.00

Hourly Rate Formula

$$\frac{\text{Estimated Annual Expenses} + \text{Estimated Annual Income}}{\text{Number of Billable Hours Worked Per Year}} = \text{Hourly Rate Required}$$

Base Figures:
Estimated annual expenses = $37,000
Desired annual income = $45,000
Number of billable hours per year = 1,000

$$\frac{\$37,000 + \$45,000}{1000} = \textbf{\$82.00 (Required Hourly Rate)}$$

If the hourly rate is higher than the market will bear:
1. Decrease annual expenses (overhead).
2. Decrease your desired annual profit.
3. Increase billable hours.

Example A (decreasing overhead):
Estimated annual expenses = $30,000 (**decrease**)
Desired annual income = $45,000
No. of billable hours per year = 1,000
Result: Required Hourly Rate will decrease to <u>$75.00</u>

Example B (decreasing desired annual profit):
Estimated annual expenses = $37,000
Desired annual income = $40,000 (**decrease**)
No. of billable hours per year = 1,000
Result: Required Hourly Rate will decrease to <u>$77.00</u>

Example C (increasing billable hours):
Estimated annual expenses = $37,000
Desired annual income = $45,000
No. of billable hours per year = 1,500 (**increase**)
Result: Required Hourly Rate will decrease to <u>$54.67</u>

NOTE: Billable hours can be increased by working longer hours or by hiring employees. If you hire employees to increase your billable hours, your annual expenses will also increase. If you decrease your annual income, taxes will decrease. Be sure to adjust your figures accordingly.

Cash to be Paid Out Worksheet
Explanation of Categories

1. Start-Up Costs

These are the costs incurred by you to get your business underway. They are generally one-time expenses and are capitalized for tax purposes.

2. Inventory Purchases

Cash to be spent during the period on items intended for resale. If you purchase manufactured products, this includes the cash outlay for those purchases. If you are the manufacturer, include labor and materials on units to be produced.

3. Variable Expenses (selling, direct)

These are the costs of all expenses that will directly relate to your product or service (other than manufacturing costs or purchase price of inventor).

4. Fixed Expenses (administrative, indirect)

Include all expected costs of office overhead. If certain bills must be paid ahead, include total cash outlay even if covered period extends into the next year.

5. Assets (long-term purchases)

These are the capital assets that will be depreciated over a period of years (land, buildings, vehicles, equipment). Determine how you intend to pay for them and include all cash to be paid out in the current period.

6. Liabilities

What are the payments you expect to make to retire any debts or loans? Do you have any Accounts Payable as you begin the new year? You will need to determine the amount of cash outlay that needs to be paid in the current year. If you have a car loan for $20,000 and you pay $500 per month for 12 months, you will have a cash outlay of $6,000 for the coming year.

7. Owner Equity

This item is frequently overlooked in planning cash flow. If you, as the business owner, will need a draw of $2000 per month on which to live, you must plan for $24,000 cash flowing out of your business. Failure to plan for this will result in a cash flow shortage and may cause your business to fail.

Note: Be sure to use the same time period throughout this worksheet.

ABC Company
Cash to be Paid Out Worksheet
(Cash Flowing Out of the Business)

Time Period Covered: Jan 1 - Dec 31, 1996

1. START-UP COSTS		1,450
Business License	30	
Corporation Filing	500	
Legal Fees	920	
Other startup costs:		
a.		
b.		
c.		
2. INVENTORY PURCHASES		
Cash out for goods intended for resale		32,000
3. VARIABLE EXPENSES (SELLING)		
Advertising/Marketing	8,000	
Freight	2,500	
Fulfillment of Orders	800	
Packaging costs	0	
Sales Salaries/Commissions	14,000	
Travel	1,550	
Miscellaneous	300	
TOTAL SELLING EXPENSES		27,150
4. FIXED EXPENSES (ADMIN)		
Financial Administration	1,800	
Insurance	900	
Licenses and Permits	100	
Office Salaries	16,300	
Rent Expense	8,600	
Utilities	2,400	
Miscellaneous	400	
TOTAL ADMINISTRATIVE EXPENSE		30,500
5. ASSETS (LONG-TERM PURCHASES)		6,000
Cash to be paid out in current period		
6. LIABILITIES		
Cash outlay for retiring debts, loans		9,900
and/or accounts payable		
7. OWNER EQUITY		
Cash to be withdrawn by owner		24,000
TOTAL CASH TO BE PAID OUT		**$131,000**

Formula for Manufacturers

Number of units produced per year x $\boxed{\text{Cost of labor for one unit plus cost of materials for one unit}}$ + Estimated Annual Expenses + Desired Annual Income

——————————————————————————————————————— = **Wholesale Price Required Per Unit**

Number of units to be produced per year

Base figures:
Cost of labor = $2.50
Cost of materials = $2.50
No. of units produced per year = 10,000
Estimated annual expenses = $93,250
Desired annual income = $50,000

$$\frac{10{,}000 \times [\$2.50 + \$2.50] + \$93{,}250 + \$50{,}000}{10{,}000} = \text{Required Wholesale Price}$$

$$\frac{\$50{,}000 + \$93{,}250 + \$50{,}000}{10{,}000} = \textbf{\$19.33 Wholesale Price Per Unit}$$

If the wholesale price is higher than the market will bear:
1. Increase the number of units produced per year.
2. Decrease the cost of labor and/or materials per unit.
3. Lower the annual expenses.
4. Decrease your desired annual profit.

Example A (increasing number of units produced per year):
Cost of labor = $2.50
Cost of materials = $2.50
No. of units produced per year = 15,000 (**increase**)
Estimated annual expenses = $110,000 (**will increase with production**)
Desired annual income = $50,000
Result: Required Wholesale Price Per Unit will decrease to $15.67

Example B (decreasing cost of labor and materials per unit):
Cost of labor = $2.25 (**decrease**)
Cost of materials = $2.00 (**decrease**)
No. of units produced per year = 10,000
Estimated annual expenses = $93,250
Desired annual income = $50,000
Result: Required Wholesale Price Per Unit will decrease to $18.58

NOTE: As employees are hired, you will incur additional overhead costs. With increased production, the cost of materials may drop because of quantity buying. Take this into consideration and adjust your figures accordingly.

Promotion

Timing of Market Entry

You won't find much written on timing of market entry, and yet it is critical to the success of your business. It is not wise to present your business to the market just because you are ready. The moment when you open your doors for business takes careful planning and research. Having your products and services available at the right time and in the right place is more a matter of understanding your customers than of your organizational schedule.

Many businesses are seasonal in nature. Since most games are purchased as Christmas gifts, the board game example we used previously would be best introduced in September and October in order to be established by the Christmas season. The marketing schedule for the gift industry is different than that of a business that sells throughout the year.

Food purchasing usually takes place around the end of the week. This is why most in-store food taste tests are done on Friday, Saturday and Sunday. Payday for most people is at the end of the week on a biweekly schedule. Promote your take-home or delivered "home-cooked" food on Friday when you know your target market has been paid, is tired at the end of the work week, is hungry and doesn't want to cook or go out! A satisfied customer will call you at other times during the week.

The way in which your customers perceive new products and services can be affected by the seasons, the weather and the holidays. Early

January and early September seem to be the best times to mail flyers and catalogs. The holiday season is over and consumers are receptive to the new year and new ideas in early January. By early September, vacations are over and children are back in school. There is more time available to look at printed material.

The major gift shows are held in the summer months (June, July and August) and again in January and February. Most wholesale buying takes place at these shows. You will want to present your products to a manufacturer's representative well before these dates.

November and December are not good months for introducing new service businesses unless they relate in some way to the holiday season. The spring is a better time to introduce a new service business.

Marketers must adjust timing of market entry according to the nature of their businesses and customers. Information from the trade journals and trade associations in your field will give you the information you will need regarding the timing patterns of your industry.

Advertising

Advertising is defined by Webster as "printed or spoken matter that tells about or praises a product or service publicly so as to make people want to buy it." Advertising is a natural extension of your marketing research and planning. It is the means for getting information about your product or service to the buying public. There are a variety of ways to accomplish this.

Advertising can remind customers and prospects about the benefits of your product or service. By now you will have identified what is **unique** about your business and how that uniqueness will **benefit the customer**. This theme or image for your product or service will carry through all of your advertising and promotion. It is what sets you apart from the competition and it is what will attract the customer. Find the inherent drama in what you are doing. Create an interest. Transfer that inherent drama into a meaningful benefit. Consumers are attracted by benefits. Your methods of advertising can establish and maintain your image, enhance your reputation, attract new customers and replace lost ones.

Publicity: Any non-paid, news-oriented presentation of a product, service or business entity in a mass media format.

Advertising allows you to have complete control. Unlike publicity, you have the final word in determining where, when and how often your message will appear, how it will look and what it will say.

Advertising takes planning, time, persistence and money. The true effectiveness of advertising is measured over time. Your target market must be repeatedly reminded of the benefits of doing business with you. This repetition has a cumulative effect. Customers will see you as an established business. Use the Advertising Worksheet (p. 106) at the end of this chapter as you plan which types of advertising methods will be used, how much they will cost and when they will be used. The planning process is like drawing a blueprint. First design the framework, next fill in the details and then begin to build the advertising plan.

Through the design of your advertising, the image and identity of your business can be set. After you have determined which forms of media you will use in your advertising campaign, decide on the format you want to use and the theme you wish to project. Each type of media will have professionals to help you. Good ads rely on the "three I's":

1. **Involve** the audience by inviting them to participate, by arousing their curiosity, by convincing them that they need your product or service.

2. **Inform** the customer about the benefits and uniqueness of your product or service in terms that they can understand. The ad must also let the customer know how, where and when the item or service can be purchased.

3. **Illustrate** the benefits through words, images or sounds that get the audience's attention and convey your information.

A good ad arouses curiosity, illustrates the benefits of using the product or service, invites the viewer to participate and tells the customer how, where and when the item may be purchased and used. With this in mind, we will now examine different types of advertising.

Newspaper advertising usually reaches a large audience, has a short life span, is relatively inexpensive and is quickly and easily changed. Tailor your ad to the editorial "mood" of the paper. Determine what special feature sections are being planned by calling the newspaper's editorial and advertising staffs. If the paper is planning to do a special feature on "desktop publishing" and you will be opening a mobile repair service for such equipment, you may want to advertise in that section. Your ad can be placed to reach a selected audience; the people reading that section will be interested in desktop publishing and in your business.

The cost of the ad will vary according to frequency of publication and area of circulation. Ads are available in various sizes and in several formats, such as display or classified ads. Analyze the advertising of your competition regarding size, placement and frequency. Your questionnaires and market research will have indicated the newspapers read by your target market. Those are the ones in which you will place your advertising.

Radio advertising is usually local, reaches a preselected audience, can be changed frequently, is limited to brief copy, is relatively expensive and can be repeated frequently. It is priced according to length of message, time of broadcast and frequency of broadcast. It is either read live by broadcasters or taped in advance.

There are two types of radio programming: background and foreground. Background programs are on the music stations. Foreground programs are on the news/talk stations. Foreground programs involve more active listeners who will probably pay more attention to your commercials.

It has been proven that you must catch the listener's attention in the first three seconds. Your ad will be done live or taped in advance. The three biggest complaints about radio commercials are that they are noisy, they have inane humor and they lack sincerity. Keep that in mind if you write your own commercial. Be simple and straightforward. Another approach to radio coverage of your business would be to offer your service as an expert in your field on a radio talk show. You can answer questions from listeners and tell about your business.

Television advertising reaches large marketing areas, is relatively expensive and is limited to brief copy. This form of advertising is usually highly professional and is priced according to length of message, time of broadcast, frequency of broadcast, time of year and whether or not the station is an independent or a member of a network.

Cost of advertising is based on gross rating points (GRP). One point equals one percent of the television sets in the TV marketing area. The GRP unit cost is determined by the competitive situation, size of area and time of year. Advertising costs may be higher during the holiday season, which is considered to be October through December. Prime time covers the period from 8:00 to 11:00 P.M. and is more costly. The "fringe time" before and after prime time may be more cost-effective for you. Don't discount cable television. This medium is becoming very useful to the small business owner. In many communities, low cost seminars are presented to instruct you in developing your own cable television ads or programs.

You need to know which media are most likely to influence your target audience and which reporters cover your kind of business. The public library has media source books available which list newspapers, magazines, radio and television stations. Find out what shows your customers watch. Television stations will have demographic and psychographic breakdowns of their viewing audiences. Most use market studies to effectively help position advertising where it will be seen by those interested in the products or services offered.

Publicity

In addition to paid advertising, don't overlook publicity. Publicity has been defined as "free advertising." Research print media, television and radio stations in your area with the help of your local library. Media references available in the library will provide you with a listing of sources and contact names. Call programmers for the radio and television talk programs and editors for the newspapers and magazines in your area. Ask if they will be doing a feature on your area of expertise. If they are, offer your services as an expert working in that field. You may be interviewed and profiled, you may be able to submit an article for publication or you may wish to place some targeted advertising to coincide with the feature. If no feature is being planned, suggest why this would be a timely topic and would be of interest to their audiences.

It is not enough to just tell about your business. You must be prepared to present a unique angle. You must convince the editor or programmer that what you have to say will appeal and will be of interest to his or her readers, listeners and viewers. For example, the book, *Chase's Calendar of Events*, lists "Homemade Bread Day" as November 17 and "Johnny Appleseed's Birthday" as September 26. The restaurant in our example could propose a feature on homemade bread to the editor of the Food Section. This marketing idea could be expanded to include a story on how the restaurant will be featuring unusual breads during the day, will provide recipes for the column and will be open for a photo opportunity on the baking of bread in the restaurant. Along the same line, Johnny Appleseed's Birthday could generate a feature on types of apples, apple recipes and an apple-tasting session.

The information you submit and the ideas with which you approach the media must be timely, important and interesting to a large segment of that media's audience.

You may wish to submit a **press release** in order to let people know who you are and what you have to offer. When preparing a press release, the two primary concerns are content and structure. News releases should be as short as possible while containing all of the important facts. Make every effort to write it in good journalistic style. Read news releases in your target news outlets and study format and content. News writing follows the "inverted pyramid" style in which every paragraph is considered more important than the ones following it. The story is written in descending order of importance. That means that the news is up front. A busy reader whose interest is not caught in the first paragraph will not read the second one. Instructions for developing a news release (see p. 107) are included at the end of this chapter.

Keep in mind that newsrooms are busy places and whoever reads your news release will be someone in a hurry. That person must be able to tell at a glance that there is something newsworthy in your release. You may wish to send a **news memo** to suggest a story idea or announce an event. The format for a news memo (p.109) is outlined at the end of this chapter.

Your business may qualify for a **Public Service Announcement** (PSA). This is a good way to announce classes or to publicize any meetings at which you may be a guest speaker. Call the media to determine its guidelines and deadlines for this type of submission.

Alternative Marketing

In addition to advertising and publicity, there are other means of getting the message about your business to your customers. **Displays** may be set up at community-oriented functions such as city fairs, community events and civic meetings. This is a good way to present your product or service to the buying public. You can also get valuable feedback. **Community involvement** can be an effective means of advertising. Membership in civic organizations can pave the way to being a guest speaker. Active membership affords you the opportunity for networking. **Networking** is the exchange of ideas and information that takes place everyday in your life. You are going to direct that exchange to your benefit and to the benefit of those around you. The more you meet with people, the more you will be able to promote your business, to learn more about the business community around you and to become more self-confident. Membership in civic and business organizations such as the chamber of commerce is an excellent means of accomplishing this.

Participation in **trade shows** and **exhibits** allows you to take advantage of promotional campaigns that would be too expensive for a small business to undertake alone. You can request listings of trade events from malls and convention centers. Participation in trade shows and membership in trade organizations give you visibility in your business field.

These shows are usually attended only by those interested in your particular field. This is an excellent way to reach your target market. You may choose to participate in a co-op display to cut costs. Co-op is a cost-sharing arrangement in which complementary service providers and/or product manufacturers share the costs of exhibit registration, booth creation, staffing and promotion. For example, the inventor of the Stock Market board game could co-op with other toy and game inventors and manufacturers for a display booth at the annual Invention Convention. Ocean Adventures could co-op with a sporting good store at a community fair. By sharing costs, the business owner is able to make better use of money allocated for trade shows and exhibits.

Brochures are essential for any business for which a prospective customer needs detailed information. More information can be supplied in a brochure than would be practical in a classified ad. Brochures can be distributed through the mail, delivered door-to-door, or passed out at fairs, mall events or conventions. An outline to help you develop a brochure has been included at the end of this section. (See p. 110.)

Direct mail can be an effective way to deliver specific information in a personal way to large numbers of people. Direct mail can take the form of inexpensive fact sheets, letters, promotional give-aways, contests, discount coupons and brochures. It can be used to solicit mail-order or phone-order business, to announce new products or services, to notify customers of price changes, to welcome new customers, to thank current customers and to announce special events such as sales. To be cost-effective, you must target your market. Rent a good list from a list broker. The principles of direct mail that were discussed in Chapter 3 also apply here. Please refer to that section for additional information.

Telemarketing can be an effective method for reaching your customers. Even when personal selling is essential, you don't have to be standing in front of the customer. You can get results by phone. The telephone can be used to contact new customers, to maintain contact with current customers, and to remind slow payers personally. To be effective, telemarketing must be organized. Use targeted lists. Make a clear and specific offer. One advantage to telemarketing is that you will get an instant response. Refer to Chapter 3 for more information on marketing by telephone.

Yellow page listings can be an effective means of promoting your product or service. They are the most widely used form of advertising. Every person with a phone has a copy of the yellow pages. You have a captive audience; they are looking at the directory because they are interested in what you have to offer.

You must decide if your business will benefit from yellow page marketing by answering the following questions:

1. In order to locate a product or service such as yours, would customers look in the yellow page section of the phone directory?

2. Are your competitors using yellow page advertising?

3. What percentage of your competitors' business comes to them as a result of yellow page advertising?

4. Can your budget afford this type of advertising? Yellow-page advertising is expensive, is contracted to on an annual basis, and is billed monthly.

If you decide that yellow page advertising should be included in your overall marketing plan, you will have to consider the following:

1. Determine the publication schedule for the directories in your area. Directories are published at various times of the year and require a few months lead time for ad placement.

2. Choose which directory or directories will best reach your target market. Most areas now have a number of competing yellow page books.

3. Determine the directory categories in which you will list your product or service. For example, our restaurant, which features take-out food, would want to be listed under "Food—carry out" and "Restaurants."

4. Decide on format, size, type, style and design of the ad. Create a strong awareness for your advertising message.

5. Compose the wording for your ad. Zero in on what is unique about your business and how you benefit your customer.

You may choose to design your own ad. The telephone company advertising staff can help you in designing an ad that will present your business in an effective manner. Before placing your ad, determine if your advertising budget can support the added monthly expense.

Discounts are another way to get additional customers. Discounts can be given to new customers and to customers who bring in referrals. They may also be offered through coupons and brochures. Everyone likes to think that they are saving money.

Promotional gimmicks in the form of T-shirts, pens, key rings, plastic shopping bags, calendars, balloons and bumper stickers can also get your name in front of the public. The most effective promotional materials are useful items. They should be appropriate to the business that they represent. For example, a logo or business name on a T-shirt is an effective way of advertising a business dealing with the out-of-doors such as a bicycle shop or a kite maker. Pens would be a good item for a manufacturer of note cards and stationery. Balloons could represent a company specializing in children's items. Be creative in your use of this advertising form.

Marketing on the Internet

Technology is affecting virtually every business. Many companies are rushing to develop "home pages" and to put their brochures and catalogs online so customers can browse, select products, ask questions, and place orders through their home or office computers. The Internet may be a great way to serve your current customers or to attract new ones.

The wise business owner will approach this rapidly developing method of marketing by first asking some key questions. What message do you want to deliver? How do you want to format the material? Who do you want to reach? Do your customers have PCs, modems, and online services?

Become familiar with online marketing while the opportunity is still in its infancy. Your decision to use this form of marketing should be an educated one.

Summary

Deciding how much money to spend to market your product or service and when and where to spend it can be difficult decisions. Choose the types of advertising that will best reach your target market. Decide which methods you can afford. Carefully plan your advertising budget and work out a cash flow statement. It is important to know how much money is needed and when it is needed. Advertising costs are an investment in your company's future.

All forms of advertising and publicity must be evaluated for effectiveness. To help you with this analysis, an Advertising Response Record (p. 111) and a Publicity Tracking Record (p. 112) have been included at the end of this section. From this information, determine what has been the most effective means of advertising for your business. Eliminate those methods which have not proven effective and transfer those funds to a more productive area. After evaluating the different methods of advertising, work up an individual plan for your business. A sample plan for a fictional company, Ocean Adventures, has been included at the end of this chapter. (See pp. 113 - 114.)

Resources

Books

Baber, Anne, and Lynne Waymon, *Great Connections: Small Talk and Networking for Businesspeople* (Manassas, VA: Impact, 1991).

Bade, Nicholas E. *Marketing Without Money* (NTC Publishing Group, 1994).

Burnett, Ed. *The Complete Direct Mail List Handbook* (Englewood Cliffs, NJ: Prentice-Hall, 1988).

Burton, Philip Ward. *Which Ad Pulled Best?* (NTC Publishing Group, 1994).

Ellesworth, Jill H. and Matthew Ellsworth. *The Internet Business Book* (New York: Wiley, 1994).

Fletcher, Tana. *Getting Publicity* (Bellingham, WA: Self-Counsel Press, 1996).

Gerson, Richard. *Marketing Strategies for Small Businesses* (San Francisco: Crisp Publications, 1994).

McHatton, Robert. *Increasing Sales and Profits with Telemarketing* (New York: Wiley, 1988).

Miller, Steve. *How to Get the Most Out of Trade Shows* (NTC Publishing Group, 1994).

Pesmen, Sandra. *Writing for the Media* (Lincolnwood, IL: NTC Publishing Co., 1983).

Phillips, Michael, and Salli Rasberry. *Marketing without Advertising* (Berkeley, CA: Nolo Press, 1990).

Price, Jeffrey. *Yellow Pages Advertising: How to Get the Greatest Return on Your Investment* (Pacific Palisades, CA: Jeffrey Price & Associates, 1991).

Yudkin, Marcia, *Six Steps to Free Publicity* (Plume/Penguin, 1994).

References

Chase, William D., and Helen, Chase. *Chase's Calendar of Events* (Chicago: Contemporary Books, annual).

Agencies

Direct Marketing Association
1120 Avenue of the Americas
New York, NY 10036
(212) 768-7277

National Mail Order Association
2807 Polk Street NE
Minneapolis, MN 55418
(612) 788-1673

R. L. Polk
431 Howard Street
Detroit, MI 48231
(313) 961-9470

Rents direct mail lists.

U.S. Small Business Administration
P.O. Box 46521
Denver, CO 80201
(800) 827-5722 (SBA Small Business Answer Desk)

Advertising MT11...$1.00

Advertising Worksheet

Name of business: Ace Sporting Goods

1. What are the features and benefits of my product or service?
Knowledgeable trained staff; open until 9 P.M. weekdays, 1-5 P.M. Sunday; full sports product line, specializing in fishing gear; offer flytying and fly fishing classes; in-house guarantee of sports equipment.

2. Who is my audience?
Youth, high school, university students
Active, middle-income sports enthusiasts
Live within 10-mile radius.

3. Who is my competition and how do they advertise?
Smith Sporting Goods - radio ads KLXY
Mailing of flyers - newspaper ad - Sunday supplement
Promotions - caps, T-shirts

4. What are the goals of my advertising campaign?
Reach high school and university market
Reach youth market
Reach fishing enthusiasts

5. How much do I plan to invest for advertising?
$1,300 per month

6. What advertising methods will I use?

X Newspapers	__ Magazines	X Yellow pages
__ Radio	__ Television	X Direct mail
__ Telemarketing	X Flyers	__ Brochures
X Coupons	__ Press release	X Promo items
X Other Youth team sponsorship		

7. When will I use them and what will they cost?
Newspaper: start 1/3/96 weekly ad x 5 $300/mo.
Direct mail flyers: 1/7/96 and 1/14/96 $550 total
Youth team: 1/26/96 $150/mo.
Promo items: 1/16/96 $100/mo.
Yellow page ad: 1/25/96 (March directory) $200/mo.

8. How will I measure the effectiveness of the advertising plan?
A. Ask customers how they heard about the store.
B. Compare cost/income on Advertising Response Record
   1. Change or delete methods that cost more than income generated.
   2. Adjust or increase budget to include radio ad, brochure, larger yellow pages and newspaper ads.

News Release Instructions

IDENTIFICATION: The business sending the release should be plainly identified. Use your letterhead or printed news release forms. The name and telephone number of a contact person for additional information must appear at the top of the page.

RELEASE DATE: Most releases should be "immediate" or "for use upon receipt." Designate a release time only if there is a specific reason such as a scheduled speech, meeting, news announcement or planned event.

MARGINS: Leave wide margins and space at the top so the editor can edit and include notations.

HEADLINES: The headline you submit should be to summarize your writing. The media will generally create their own headline.

LENGTH: When double spaced, most press releases are one to two pages in length. If you have a longer release, write the highlights into an attached news memo and include the news release as background material.

STYLE: Use the summary lead and the five Ws (who, what, when, where, why and, sometimes, how.) Double space. Use short sentences with active verbs. Make sure it is accurate, timely and not self-serving. Try to use an objective style of writing. If you must use more than one page, do not split a paragraph from the first to second page. Center the word "more" at the bottom of the first page.

CHECK AND DOUBLECHECK: Proofread names, spellings, numbers and grammar carefully.

PLACEMENT: Your news release should be in the hands of editors well in advance of deadlines. Contact the city desk, assignment editor or feature editor with whom you are working to clarify deadlines and publication schedules.

END: Put "30" or ### at the end of the press release.

News releases should be cleanly typed on 8$\frac{1}{2}$ x 11 inch white paper. They should be hand-delivered or mailed First Class to the designated media contact.

News Release Sample

(PRINT ON COMPANY LETTERHEAD OR PRESS RELEASE FORM)

PRESS RELEASE

February 7, 1996   Contact: David Blair

For Immediate Release   (555) 613-7965

FLY FISHING DEMONSTRATION AND CONTEST

John Bacon, well-known local fly-fisherman, will demonstrate techniques for dry and wet fly casting and will judge a contest to be held in the parking lot of Ace Sporting Goods on Saturday, February 19, 1996 from 10 A.M. to 4 P.M.

Ace's owner, David Blair, stated that the popularity of the book and movie, *A River Runs Through It,* has led to an increased interest in the sport of fly fishing. Blair announced that the fee for participation in the contest is $5, with all of the proceeds going to the Memorial Hospital Children's Wing. All contestants will receive a ten percent discount coupon from the sporting goods store.

After receiving instructions from Mr. Bacon, contestants will be judged on form, distance and accuracy. Prizes include theater passes, dinner coupons and sporting event tickets. The contest is open to everyone. Information and pre-registration are available at Ace Sporting Goods, 271 Adams St., Blair, NY, or by phoning (555) 613-7965.

-30-

News Memo Format

(PRINT ON LETTERHEAD OR NEWS MEMO FORM)

TO: Addressed to editor or reporter.

FROM: Your name, address and phone number.

RE: A one or two sentence statement regarding the story you are suggesting, the event to which you are inviting reporters, the meeting, class or seminar you have scheduled, or other purpose of the news release.

TIME AND DATE: Specific time, date, year of event or of submission release.

LOCATION: Specific location, including directions if the location is not well known or easily found.

WHY: You must have a reason for the news release or the event.

CONTACT: The name and phone number of someone the news editor or reporter can contact with questions about the news release.

Developing a Brochure

A brochure is a general term for promotional material that tells the following about your business:

1. **Business name.**

2. **Business address**. Be sure to include the full address and zip code.

3. **Telephone number**. Be sure to include the area code.

4. **Name of a contact person**. Customers prefer to ask for an individual when they call.

5. **Photos or drawings** of your product or a representation of your service.

6. **Description of your product or service.**

7. **Price list**. Indicate whether price is wholesale or retail. Indicate any quantity discounts.

8. **Terms of payment**.

   Net 30: Invoice must be paid in full within 30 days.

   Net 30, 2%/10: Invoice to be paid in full in 30 days. If paid within 10 days, a 2% discount can be taken on the bill, excluding the shipping charges.

   C.O.D.: "Cash on delivery;" invoice is to be paid to the delivery agent on receipt of the goods.

   ProForma: Goods will be shipped after receipt of full payment.

9. **Return Policy:** You may wish to include a statement as follows: "Returns and/or adjustments must be made within 14 days of receipt of goods." Use a time frame of your choice.

10. **Shipping terms:** F.O.B. Origin would mean that the customer pays shipping charges and assumes the responsibility for the goods from the time they leave your business. Example: FOB Tustin, CA.

11. **Minimum order policy:** Can be a dollar or unit amount.

12. **Warranty and/or guarantee.**

Advertising Response Record

Company Name: __Ace Sporting Goods—January 1996__

Type of Ad	Date Run	Cost	Circulation	No. Responses	Income Generated
Register newspaper 2" x 4" in sports section	Weekly 1/3, 1/10, 1/17, 1/24, 1/31	$300.00	15,000	end of month coupon responses - 264 phone orders - 26	$6,600.00 $520.00
Flyers with 10% discount coupon - high school, university	Mailed 1/7/96	$350.00	750	10	$260.00
Flyers with 10% discount for fishermen	Mailed 1/14/96	$200.00	500	96	$1,152.00
Youth team sponsorship caps/shirts with store name	1/26/96	$150.00	12	6 team members purchased equipment at 20% discount	$135.00

Publicity Tracking Record

Company Name: __Home-Cookin Food Delivery__

Media Name	Contact Person	Address	Date	Material Sent	Follow-Up	Response	Results	Notes
KRTZ Radio "News about Town"	Jim Bell Prog. Dir. 266-8761	722 Main St. Baker, MD 20601	1/8/96	News Memo Promo Kit	1/15 - phoned Delivered dinner	1/17 - booked for 2/7 talk show 5-6 P.M.	12 calls taken on air; 160 responses for flyer.	Focus: Delivered dinners for Valentine's Day. Holiday menus.
Tribune newspaper	Ann Mead Editor 254-3208	621 6th St. Baker, MD 20603	1/9/96	Press Release Promo Kit	1/15 - phoned Delivered Valentine Cake	1/18 - submit 6 recipes and article by 2/5	Article printed 2/10; 200 responses for flyers.	Focus: Valentine recipes
Orange City magazine	Karen Brown Reporter 201-8960	724 Adams Baker, MD 20603	1/9/96	Promo Kit Photo	1/15 - phoned	Not interested at this time.		Focus: Unique area business
Metro Cable Evening News	David Kim Prog. Dir. 249-6201	2664 Bryan Baker, MD 20601	2/20/96	Promo Kit Photo	2/27 - phoned	Will film food delivery 6 P.M. on 3/6		Focus: Unique local business
ABC Local P.M. News	Steve Douglas Prog. Dir. 865-0210	819 17th St. Allen, MD 28104	2/28/96	Promo on Fair News memo	3/6 - phoned	Will film 5 min. segment for 6 P.M. news 3/30		Focus: Baker City Food Fair

Sample Advertising Plan
Advertising Ideas for Ocean Adventures

RADIO: Contact local radio stations and ask for their procedures in securing talk show guests. Inform them of your area of expertise and stress the uniqueness of what you offer and the high interest of the public in what your business is doing. Suggest that you can relate kayaking experiences that you have had and would enjoy taking listener calls.

NEWSPAPER: Contact the sports editor, business editor and travel editor and slant your article idea according to their areas of interest. The sports editor would be interested in an article about "The Sport of Ocean Kayaking." The business editor may want to cover a new and unique business developing within the area covered by his newspaper. The travel editor will be interested in an article entitled, "Kayaking to Baja." Have black and white photos available of the different aspects of your business.

Consider publishing an ad in the business section. Trained people at the newspaper can advise you about ad placement and size. Be prepared to give the who, what, why, where and how of the class or trip you will be offering.

TELEVISION: Contact television studios in your area and inquire about their format for securing talk show guests. Suggest that you could demonstrate the use of a kayak for their viewers, tell about trips you have taken and demonstrate safety techniques. Perhaps, the host would be willing to be televised while taking a basic lesson.

Cable television also offers opportunities for coverage and less expensive advertising. Explore this resource.

Public Broadcasting Stations often have televised auctions as fundraisers. Consider donating your Basic Paddling Course as one of the items offered for auction. This would be invaluable advertising.

DISPLAY: Create a display featuring photos of your trips and classes, copies of any publicity you have received, a kayak and the gear related to its use. Have plenty of brochures and business cards on hand. Be prepared to answer questions regarding your business. Community affairs such as fairs and festivals usually offer low cost space for this type of display. This format can also be used as an exhibit at trade shows such as a Travel Show or Sports and Boating Show. These larger events are usually held in sports arenas or convention facilities. Listings of such events are available from the Chamber of Commerce and convention centers.

COMMUNITY INVOLVEMENT: Join the Chamber of Commerce or other civic organization. This will afford you a forum for speaking as well as providing networking opportunities. Consider working with a Scout Council. You could counsel in kayaking, water safety and/or marine studies. This offers a new area for networking. Look into teaching through the YMCA/YWCA. Basic skills courses could be taught through the Y with a discount given to students who continue study privately.

BROCHURE: Make your message personal and stress your product or service. A brochure should show how your business is different from the competition and stress the advantages of dealing with you. (See guidelines for brochure development on p. 110.)

YELLOW PAGE AD: Discuss placement and category with the staff in the advertising department of the yellow pages. They will be able to advise you regarding timing and costs of this type of advertising.

PROMOTIONAL GIMMICKS: T-shirts with your name and logo could be given to those attending your classes and going on your trips. This would seem to be an appropriate promotional tool; active, outdoor people wear t-shirts and you will get good exposure that way.

Note: Advertising is a continuing process. Be prepared to follow up on all leads. Have brochures ready to be mailed when you receive an inquiry. People get distracted and lose interest if their requests aren't handled promptly. Consider discounts for groups and referrals.

Packaging

Two elements are involved in determining the impression you wish to make about your business: image and identity. **Image** refers to the emotional or psychological feeling a customer has about your business. Does the environmental newsletter publisher use recycled paper which shows a commitment to the environment? Will the take-out food restaurant prepare special foods for individuals on diets? Will the dry cleaning establishment open at 7:30 A.M. for the convenience of customers? A company creates a good and lasting image by listening to customers and by being willing to meet their needs. **Identity** refers to the objective interpretation by a customer of how you compare to the competition, of how stable or established you are and of where your company is positioned. It also involves the development of recognizable visual materials that will help promote your company. If natural color paper, green ink and an owl logo are used for the environmental newsletter, for the company's brochure and on the company's truck sign, the public will soon recognize that company when they see these items. This chapter will explore image and identity and show how packaging and promotional materials can have an impact on the success of your business. A creative image combined with distinctive packaging will enable consumers to single out your product or service in a crowd.

Graphic Identity

First impressions are lasting, and often the first impression made by a business is through its graphic identity. Graphic identity refers to the visual representation of your company. It is the design of your logo, the sign on your store, the uniforms of your employees, the style of your promotional materials and the packaging of your product or service.

A company's graphic or visual identity usually includes a logo, a logotype (type style) and company colors. The combinations you choose will create your identity and will make your promotional and packaging materials recognizable. In today's highly competitive world, it is important to be recognized, to be remembered and to be viewed as an established business.

A **logo** is a symbol that represents the company. It may be a monogram of the company's initials or a design. A logo is a quick way of getting people to notice and remember your business. When designing your logo, you want to be sure that it is appropriate to your business and that the art work is timely. You can design your own, select from standard logos available at a print shop, hire a professional artist, or work with a high school or college art student. Be sure to consider registering your logo with the Copyright Office or the Patent and Trademark Office in Washington, DC. Refer to Chapter 2 regarding these protections.

Logotype refers to the type style used in the writing of your business name. The type size, placement and style can communicate a great deal about your company. For example, a capitalized bold typeface may project the image of an aggressive company with a foothold in the marketplace. It would inspire confidence. However, a delicate pastel script would not be appropriate for or inspire confidence in a construction company!

There are hundreds of type styles and sizes available and, within each type family, there are basic, italic and bold versions.

Often a company will wish to adopt **company colors**. Most often two colors are used. Just as with typestyle, the colors you choose can set the tone for your marketing materials. Make sure the colors you choose fit your company and the identity you wish to project. The addition of color to your printed material will increase the cost. Be sure to adjust your marketing budget accordingly.

You may be a small company competing with larger companies or a new company entering an existing market. You need to look competent and established. A carefully planned and implemented graphic identity can give you the edge you need and should last for many years.

Promotional Materials

A company's image is based primarily on its paper correspondence. According to a survey conducted by Yankelovich, Skelly and White, corporate identity materials such as stationery, business cards and envelopes are second only to annual sales in a list of seven items that convey a company's image.

From the first day that you begin business, it will be necessary for you to have certain materials that represent your business.

Business cards are one of the most universally used marketing tools. Not only do they give your business credibility, they serve as a visual reminder of you and your business. Remember your company's image and incorporate your graphic identity when designing your card. Keep the following considerations in mind:

1. The logo must be appropriate and descriptive.

2. The company name must be legible and in the correct type size.

3. A contact person's name and phone number must appear.

4. Include a statement about the product or service offered.

5. The overall appearance of the card must be pleasing.

6. The card should be one the customer will remember.

A business card is like a mini-billboard. It should tell the what, why, who, how, when and where of your business. What is the business name, why do I need what the company provides, who do I contact at the business, how can I contact them, when are they available and where are they located?

Following is a listing of some of the most common items that your company may need and that can incorporate your graphic identity:

Brochures	Building sign
Business cards	Business reply envelopes
Checks	Contracts/agreements
Display signs	Envelopes
Flyers	Invoices
Letterhead	Mailing labels

Name badges	Presentation folders
Promotional give aways	Purchase orders
Uniforms	Vehicle sign

Expand the information formatted for your business card and develop a "look" that appears on all your promotional materials and carries over to your package design.

Package Design

Packaging serves two purposes: it protects the product and it conveys the image or identity of the business. Consumers often decide to purchase a product based upon the appeal of the package that encloses it. Attractive packaging can also lead to impulse buying. The appearance of personnel, the setting of the work location and the types of promotional materials such as signs, invoices and brochures are all forms of "packaging" used by service providers.

In order to keep costs down, many companies start out using stock packaging rather than having it custom designed. The selection of stock packaging has greatly improved in the past few years. Look through the trade magazines of the packaging industry for supplier listings and advertisements. These publications will cover new techniques and materials that are available. You may attend trade shows in order to look at samples and to review prices. The *Thomas Register* (a library reference book) and the yellow pages will list packaging suppliers.

Suppliers: Individuals or businesses that provide resources needed by a company and its competitors in order to produce goods and services.

Consider product liability, bar codes, shape and materials. Can your package be opened without risk of customer injury? Many retail stores will not handle products without bar coding. Shape is important. Storage areas and shelf space are designed for square or rectangular packaging. Materials must be chosen carefully. Some types of plastic deteriorate and become yellow and brittle with improper storage.

The package itself can be used as an advertising medium. Packaging and labeling are forms of direct communication with the consumer. The expansion of self-serve and warehouse shopping has placed increased emphasis on packaging. The package must convince the shopper to buy a particular product over that of the competition.

The Fair Packaging and Labeling Act (FPLA) is the primary federal law requiring mandatory labeling provisions for all packaged consumer commodities and outlining labeling provisions. The Food and Drug Administration has regulatory authority for enforcing the FPLA as it relates to food, drugs, cosmetics and therapeutic devices. The Federal Trade Commission has authority for all other consumer commodities. The packaging and ad labeling guidelines for your area of concern can be obtained by contacting the governmental agencies listed at the end of this chapter. The time you spend in designing your packaging and researching the materials to be used will be time well spent.

Summary

The second part of this book has been concerned with examining the five "Ps" of marketing: product, place, price, promotion and packaging. As you have seen, these areas overlap and, when viewed as a whole, work together to form a "marketing mix." You have now developed a plan for reaching the target market you identified in the first part of this book. Researching and reaching your target market are not enough. A wise and successful business owner soon learns that a customer must be retained. The third section of this book will cover the areas of customer service, customer satisfaction, community involvement and communication, and it will explore ways of retaining the target market.

Resources

Books

Beaumont, Michael, *Type, Design, Color, Character and Use* (Cincinnati, OH: North Light Books, 1987).

Bly, Robert, *Create the Perfect Sales Piece: How to Produce Brochures, Catalogs, Fliers and Pamphlets* (New York: Wiley, 1985).

Carter, David, *Designing Corporate Identity Programs for Small Corporations* (New York: Art Direction Book Company, 1982).

Selame, Elinor, and Joseph, Selame, *The Company Image: Building your Identity and Influence in the Marketplace* (New York: Wiley, 1988).

Trade Journals

Boxboard Containers
Maclean Hunter Publishing Company
29 N. Wacker Drive
Chicago, IL 60606
(312) 726-2802
Industry news about shipping containers, setup paper boxes, folding cartons and other products.

Folding Carton

E. Gilbert Mathews, Inc.
274 Tanner Marsh Road
Guilford, CT 06437
(203) 453-3963

Covers all aspects of manufacturing, printing and using carton packaging.

Food and Drug Packaging

Edgell Communications
7500 Old Oak Blvd.
Cleveland, OH 44130
(216) 826-2839

Reports industry trends, marketing innovations and regulatory matters in the packaging of food and drugs.

Forms and Label Purchasing

North American Publishing Company
401 N. Broad Street
Philadelphia, PA 19108
(215) 238-5300

Offers advice and reports on new products for buyers of business forms and labels.

Packaging

Cahners Publishing Co.
1350 E. Touhy Avenue
Des Plaines, IL 60017-5080

Reports on packaging innovations, designs, marketing, consumer protection and other subjects.

References

Packaging Marketplace

Gale Research Inc.
835 Penobscot Bldg.
Detroit, MI 48226

An extensive listing of packaging manufacturers.

Thomas Register of American Manufacturers, New York: Thomas Publishing Company, annual.

Agencies

Bureau of Consumer Protection
Division of Special Statutes
6th Street & Pennsylvania Ave., NW
Washington, DC 20580

Request information on product labeling and packaging requirements.

Consumer Products Safety Commission
Bureau of Compliance
5401 Westbard Avenue
Bethesda, MD 20207
(800) 638-2772 (Recorded message)

Request information and booklets on laws and regulations regarding packaging.

U.S. Department of Commerce
Office of Consumer Affairs
Washington, DC 20233

Request booklets such as: *Advertising, Packaging and Labeling.*

Federal Trade Commission
Office of Consumer Affairs
Washington, DC 20233

Request trade practice rules and labeling requirements that apply to your business or product line.

Food and Drug Administration
5600 Fishers Lane
Rockville, MD 20857

Contact on a federal, state and local level to determine requirements governing the packaging and labeling of food-related products.

National Institute of Standards & Technology
U.S. Department of Commerce
Gaithersburg, MD 20899

Write for information on special labeling required for products containing precious metals.

U.S. Small Business Administration
P.O. Box 46521
Denver, CO 80201
(800) 827-5722 (SBA Small Business Answer Desk)

Effective Business Communications MP1...$1.00
Promotion: Solving the Puzzle VT3...$30.00 (VHS tape with workbook)

PART III

Retaining Your Target Market

✔ **Customer Service**

✔ **Customer Satisfaction**

✔ **Communication**

Customer Service

Remember that it will cost you much more to acquire a new customer through advertising than to retain a current customer through good customer service. According to a recent study done by the American Productivity and Quality Center, 68 percent of customers stop doing business with a company if they receive poor service. Customers are five times more likely to stop doing business with a company because of poor service than because of poor product quality or too high a cost. Poor customer service does not pay.

The most common customer complaints can be broken down into three areas and are as follows:

1. **Employee-oriented:**
   Employees are not courteous.
   Employees are not attentive.
   Employees are not knowledgeable.
   Employees are not helpful.
   Employee appearance is not good.
   Slow service.

2. **Location-oriented:**
   Poor appearance of business location.
   Location is inconvenient.
   Parking is inadequate.

3. **Product/service-oriented:**
   Price is too high for value received.

Quality not as good as expected.
Failure to back up product.
Poor availability or selection of product.
Poor guarantee or warranty.

As you can see, customers can express dissatisfaction regarding your employees, your location and/or your product or service.

Employee-Oriented Complaints

The two most frequently cited customer complaints are "being ignored by salespeople" and "being treated in a rude manner." The average American company will lose 10 to 30 percent of its customers per year due to poor service. When customers have a choice, they will go to the competition almost one-third of the time. These are customers you can not afford to lose.

Successful companies realize that their strongest selling point can be high-quality service. Small businesses which put their emphasis on customer service are more likely to survive and succeed than companies that emphasize the advantages of lower price, convenience, speed of delivery or product performance. While these are important to the consumer, the personal dealings with staff can be what brings that customer back for repeat business.

Provide specific training and information so employees know exactly what to do in every situation. Lack of knowledge on the part of the employees reflects on the business owner. It is your responsibility to train and inform the staff. Make sure that they understand your company, its products and services. They must be able to locate products, explain features and understand warranty and guarantee policies of the company. They must be able to help customers make informed decisions, even if it means no immediate sale. Customers will remember that help, even if it means referring them to the competition.

There are times when a competitor's products or services might better serve a customer's needs. Don't be afraid of referrals; they go two ways. Customers will feel that you have put their needs above those of your business. They will remember and return to your company in the future. You may have "lost" one sale, but you will not have lost a customer. You will also find that your competitors appreciate the referrals and will not hesitate to return the favor when they can not meet customer's needs. For example, if your desktop publishing company is unable to take on a publishing project because of an already heavy work load, refer that customer to a competitor. Call the competitor and explain the situation and state that you know the quality of his or her work is high and that the customer will be pleased. Of course, you want to make sure that you have checked out your competition so you can be confident in making such statements and referrals.

Customers must be greeted promptly and courteously. Maintain eye contact. Make sure that personal appearance and grooming are appropriate to the business type and setting. You may want to institute a dress code or provide uniforms. This also reinforces the identity and image you have designed for your company. Go the extra mile and respond to special requests. Make sure that you stock everything needed in order to use a product. If an item you sell requires batteries in order to run, make sure you also sell batteries. Smile and say "thank you." Of course, these items apply to the business owner as well as the employee!

Location-Oriented Complaints

The appearance of your business location or work area is important to your customers. It reflects the image or identity you have adopted for your company, your products and your services. Chapter 8 contained a Location Analysis Worksheet (p. 82-83), which covered items such as traffic patterns for customers, availability of parking and safety issues such as crime rate.

Make sure that your customers know how to reach your business. Include a small map or directions for reaching your business on your brochure or flyer. Make sure that employees who may be answering the phone can give good directions to your business location. Designate the nearest parking area on your map. If you are a service business and your clients must use public parking, validate their parking tickets. The amount of money you will spend in reimbursing parking fees will seem small in comparison to the goodwill you'll generate.

Be aware of a customer's personal needs. Can you assign an employee to carry merchandise to vehicles? Look out for your customers' safety. Is your establishment and the surrounding area properly lighted? What is the condition of the pavement and sidewalk? Would your customers feel safer with a security person on the premises? Evaluating your location and its appearance in terms of your customers' needs is an ongoing process throughout the life of your business.

Product/Service-Oriented Complaints

Customers want to feel that they are getting what they pay for. Give customers the quality of product or service you would want. Put yourself in the "buyer's seat" when dealing with your customers.

In order to retain your customer base, you must always anticipate the competition. Make sure that your pricing structure is in line with that of the competition. Keep up with trends in order to be aware of new products and services you can provide.

Niche: A well-defined group of customers for which the product or service you have to offer is particularly suitable.

No business can provide all things to all people, however. Know your customer base. Understand what they are interested in purchasing and what you are comfortable with providing. Plan your business start-up and growth with the goal of establishing a niche for yourself in the marketplace. Build a reputation for depth and expertise in a selected area. By focusing on that niche, you will be able to avoid many product or service complaints. You will be aware of the needs and wants of your target market, you will be dealing with merchandise you understand, can explain, and will stand behind, and you will know when to refer customers to a competitor.

For example, the kayak instructor may establish a niche by providing kayak lessons, leading ocean-going trips and selling kayak gear. The goal is to become established as the kayaking expert. Selling tennis rackets and baseball caps would be counterproductive.

Resources

Cannie, Joan Koob. *Turning Lost Customers Into Gold . . . and the Art of Achieving* (AMACOM, 1993).

Falk, Edgar. *1001 Ideas to Create Retail Excitement* (Englewood Cliffs, NJ: Prentice-Hall, 1994).

Customer Satisfaction

Listen to your customers. You are not really selling products or services as much as you are selling customer satisfaction. Satisfied customers return to spend more money and are likely to refer new customers to you. Dissatisfied customers terminate their spending and discourage potential customers. Warranties and guarantees are the most powerful marketing statements a company can make. They are especially effective for a new company. They create a relationship that says "we stand behind our product or service."

Warranties

A **warranty** explains what the seller promises about the product being sold. It is a written statement of the manufacturer's commitment if a product is defective or performs poorly. Common law says that producers must stand behind their products. The federal Magnuson-Moss Act of 1975 states that producers must provide a "clearly written" warranty. This means stating the limits of any warranty including its length, specific areas of performance and whether it includes labor and routine maintenance. The act also requires full warranties to meet certain minimum standards, which include reasonable repairs and replacement.

The Federal Trade Commission has established guidelines to ensure that warranties are clear and definite and not deceptive or unfair. Some companies used to say their products were "fully warranted" or "absolutely guaranteed." However they didn't state the time period or spell out the meaning of the warranty. Now a company has to make clear whether it

Producers: The components of the organizational market that acquire products and service that enter into the production of products and services that are sold or supplied to others.

129

is offering a "full" or "limited" warranty and the law defines what "full" means. The warranty must also be available for inspection before the purchase.

A company that produces a product must make specific decisions about what the warranty will cover, and then the warranty should be communicated clearly to the customer.

If you are a company selling a product, you must make sure you understand the manufacturer's warranty, can explain it to your customers and know how to enforce it if product failure or dissatisfaction occurs.

Guarantees

A **guarantee** implies making oneself or one's business liable or responsible for the performance of something. It is a pledge or promise. A warranty is provided by a manufacturer. A guarantee is provided by the seller of a product or the performer of a service. Ideally the best guarantee is unconditional, easy to understand, meaningful, easy to invoke and quick to pay off.

Stand by your guarantees, no matter what. Let your customers know that your commitment to customer satisfaction is of the utmost importance to you. Adopt a liberal return policy. Some customers may abuse this policy, but your good customers will appreciate the policy and will spread the word. Word-of-mouth endorsements are the best and least expensive advertising you can get.

Making good on customer returns shouldn't be viewed solely as an expense. It is a learning opportunity. Why was the item returned? How could the return have been avoided? Did the customer feel that the matter was resolved in a timely and cordial way?

Accept responsibility for all mistakes. When an error is made on a customer's order, respond by saying, "I'm sorry for the mistake. What can I do to correct the problem to your satisfaction?" No matter how angry the customer may be, this response will usually defuse the situation. Answer all customer inquiries and complaints as promptly as possible. Meet all time commitments. Quality begins with the owner and is an ongoing process. Never stop asking how you can do better. Find out what your customer expects from your product or service. Then deliver it and guarantee it.

It has been estimated that when customers are displeased, they tell from 7 to 11 people about their dissatisfaction. But only one in 26 dissatisfied customers complains to the company offering the poor service. Providing an atmosphere and the means for allowing a customer to voice a complaint is a matter of maintaining open communication.

CHAPTER

14

Communication

If you want your business to be successful, you must listen to and talk with customers in order to learn how you might serve them better. The most successful business owners identify with and stay close to their customers. They give their customers the level of service they themselves would expect to receive. These business owners also maintain a two-way communication channel with their employees. They educate employees about the company and its products and services. They listen to employees concerns. Employees often know your customers best. Their input should be encouraged. This chapter will look at the importance of establishing ways to generate customer feedback and encourage employee communication.

Mailing Lists

Mailing lists can be developed from your own customer files. You can capture names and addresses from checks, credit cards, business cards and questionnaires. Encourage customers to drop their business cards into a basket or bowl by providing a monthly prize drawing. For customers without cards, you can provide forms to fill out.

Stay in touch. Educate your customers about a new product, alert customers about sales, introduce a new staff member or take a survey to determine customer satisfaction. If you see something that might interest them, even if it is not related to your business, write them a note or give them a call. Follow up a purchase with a phone call or a response card to make sure they are satisfied. Remember birthdays and special events by sending cards or other appropriate acknowledgments. A birthday wish is personal and has relatively little competition from other cards. Most businesses send holiday greeting cards that arrive in bunches during the holidays and the individual thought is lost in the volume of cards.

To cut the cost of mailing, consider using postcards, which you can use in the following ways:

1. Announcements: Postcards can be used to announce an address change, to introduce new personnel, to invite customers to a sale, to announce the arrival of new merchandise or to tell about the addition of an 800 number or a FAX line for faster order processing.

2. Coupons: Postcards can be sent to advertise single items, mention a special discount or offer a free item. Add the line, "Please present this coupon in order to receive...."

3. Direct mail marketing: Postcards can serve as both a promotional piece and an order form. List one or more items that customers can order by mail and include space for name, address and ordering information. Specify if payment must accompany the order.

4. Thank you notes: Postcards can demonstrate your appreciation for the customer's business.

Don't let your customers forget you!

Customer Feedback

Let customers know that you value their opinions whether good or bad. Provide ways for them to communicate with you. Most unhappy customers who do not complain will just not buy from you again. The reason they do not complain to the business owner is that they think the complaint will do no good or they aren't sure how to voice their complaint. Your job is to show the customer that complaints and comments do make a difference by setting up a straightforward method to show dissatisfaction and by letting them know when and how the problems they point out have been corrected. Some methods for encouraging customer communication include the following:

Face-to-face communication is the most effective. Listen to what customers say about you, your company and your competition. Talk and meet with your customers in order to learn about their attitudes, what they like and what they dislike. Ask questions. Share knowledge of your industry and educate them with seminars or talks about your product or service.

The **telephone** can be an effective method of communication for a small business. Personal phone contact is a good way to get information and to give explanations. Make sure that you and your employees use good telephone techniques. Always introduce yourself by giving your name as well as the name of the company that you represent. Use tact and a friendly tone. Use the words "thank you" and "appreciate" often. Successful sales people follow up with customers, usually by phone, in order to see that the purchases made or services received were satisfactory. On incoming calls, use "hold" sparingly and keep the caller informed. Some businesses with clients nationwide may find an 800 phone number a good tool for getting a prompt response.

A **complaint system** should be established to show customers that your company will listen. Post signs explaining your policy, use a suggestion box, print a customer service name and number on cards or bills. Designate someone to handle the comments and to respond when appropriate. Comment cards are often used for restaurants and other businesses with many customers whose identities are not known. Customers should be asked about problems and impressions and the comments must be noted.

Questionnaires can form the basis for face-to-face, mail and phone surveys. Make the survey short, clear and specific in order to gather meaningful information. Offer premiums such as T-shirts, mugs or discount coupons to boost the response rate. A sample questionnaire for a retail store has been included at the end of this chapter (p. 139).

Communicate with Employees

You want to also provide methods of communication for your employees. Hold regular staff meetings. Each employee can keep track of the things they would like to discuss at the meetings. These meetings provide an excellent opportunity for discussing customer complaints, reviewing new product or service ideas, and working out staff scheduling. Meetings should be held during regular work hours or be paid for as overtime after regular hours.

Consider cash rewards for employees with money-saving, money-making or time-saving ideas. This will demonstrate your interest in their ideas and input. Get your employees to help promote the company by handing out fliers, by representing the business at industry meetings or by getting involved in community events.

Community Involvement

Community involvement is another form of communication. It shows that you are committed to your business for the long haul. It demonstrates to your customers, your suppliers, your competitors, other businesses and the community, in general, that you have a vested interest in the welfare of your home and business community.

Active participation in community organizations and events can help project the identity or image you have chosen for your company. Membership in civic groups and business organizations such as the Chamber of Commerce can give you opportunities for public speaking, conference exhibiting and networking. There is strength in numbers and membership can help you have political impact. You can effect change more easily when identified with a group. The issues of health care, workers' compensation and other employee benefits are of extreme importance to business owners and membership in business organizations will allow you access to the most current information on these subjects.

Consider donating your product or service to a charitable cause. This often results in positive exposure to community leaders and civic groups. While consumer products are usually desired the most, many organizations also look for donations of professional service time. If you have a restaurant, consider hosting an event for a charitable organization. This works best if volunteers for that charity are potential customers.

Sponsorship of youth athletic teams or events such as walk-a-thons can also get visibility for your business and show your commitment.

Project an image as an integral part of your community. It is the friendly feelings people have that draw them to you and your business. It has been said that the best form of advertising is "word of mouth." The most successful businesses are based upon customer and community loyalty.

Resources

Books

Cannie, Joan, and Donald Caplin, *Keeping Customers for Life* (New York: AMACOM, 1992).

Carr, Clay, *Frontline Customer Service: Fifteen Keys to Customer Service* (New York: Wiley, 1990).

Cathcart, Jim, *Relationship Selling: the Key to Getting and Keeping Customers* (Perigree Books, Putnam Publishing Group, 1990).

Dennis, Larry, *Repeat Business* (Portland, OR: Rising Tide Publishing, 1992).

Finch, Lloyd C., *Telephone Courtesy and Customer Service* (San Francisco: Crisp Publications, 1990).

Hart, Christopher, *The Guarantee Edge* (New York: AMACOM, 1992).

LeBoeuf, Michael, *How to Win Customers and Keep Them for Life* (New York: G.P. Putnam, 1989).

Sewell, Carl, and Paul Brown, *Customers for Life* (New York: Pocket Books, 1990).

Timm, Paul, *50 Powerful Ideas You Can Use to Keep Your Customers* (Hawthorne, NJ: The Career Press, 1992).

Vavra, Terry G., *Aftermarketing: How to Keep Your Customers for Life through Relationship Marketing* (Homewood, IL: Business One Irwin, 1993).

Willingham, Ron, *Integrity Selling: How to Succeed in Selling in the Competitive Years Ahead* (New York: Doubleday, 1987).

References

The IFM Encyclopedia of Customer Relations
Institute for Management
Old Saybrook, CT 06457

300-page, loose-leaf manual that covers most facets of customer relations with enough detail to assist a company in setting up a new customer relations department.

Agencies

Federal Trade Commission
Office of Consumer Affairs
Washington, DC 20233

Request regulations and rulings that concern warranties and guarantees.

U.S. Small Business Administration
P.O. Box 46521
Denver, CO 80201
(800) 827-5722 (SBA Small Business Answer Desk)

Creative Selling: The Competitive Edge MT1...$ .50
Checklist for Developing a Training Program PM1...$ .50
Employees: How to Find and Pay Them PM2...$1.00
Marketing for Small Business: An Overview MT2...$1.00
Marketing: Winning Customers with a Workable Plan
    VT1...$30.00 (Videotape)

Sample Questionnaire - Customer Survey

In an effort to meet the needs of our customers, we have developed the following questionnaire. We hope you will take a few moments to tell us how you feel about our store, how we rate next to our competition and what we can do to improve our product line and our service.

1. Is this your first visit to our store? _____ Yes _____ No

2. What stores do you consider our closest competition?

3. What good qualities displayed by competition would you like to see in our store?

4. What do you value most about this store?
_____ Selection _____ Service _____ Pricing _____ Convenience _____ Other

5. How could our store be improved?

6. What other products or services would you like us to offer?

7. How did you first hear about our product/service?

8. What newspapers and magazines do you read regularly?

9. Which radio and television stations do you tune in to regularly?

10. Do you respond to direct mailings? _____ Yes _____ No

11. Do you use discount coupons? _____ Yes _____ No

12. Please indicate your age and sex:
_____ Male _____ Female   _____ 18-34 _____ 35-49 _____ 50-65 _____ 66+

13. Please indicate your annual household income:
_____ under $15,000 _____ $15-24,000 _____ $25-49,000
_____ $50-74,000 _____ over $75,000

Thank you for your responses. If you would like to be included in our mailings for in-store promotions and sales, please complete the following:

Name _____ Birthdate: _____ Month _____ Day _____

Address _____

City _____ State _____ Zip _____

Phone (_____)_____

Summary

By completing the work outlined in this book, you have surveyed the market and examined trends as you researched your idea for a new product or service. You have written a disclosure letter, started a journal and explored the protections offered through copyright, trademark and patent. Questionnaires have been composed, distributed and evaluated in order to get a profile of your target market and a response to the validity of your idea. You have prepared a prototype and done some market testing. Evaluation of the competition has helped you determine what is unique about your business and how it will benefit the customer. By putting together your demographic and psychographic findings, you have zeroed in on the target market.

You then examined the five "Ps" of marketing: product, place, price, promotion and packaging. You have positioned your product or service and prepared to enter the marketplace. Careful thought has been given to timing of market entry, advertising, location and distribution methods.

Finally, you looked at the three "Cs" of customer relations: customer service, customer satisfaction and communication.

The development of a marketing plan is an orderly, objective way of learning about products and services and the people who buy them. Research is limited only by your imagination. Much can be done with very little cost except for your time and mental effort. A marketing plan incorporates the three parts of this book. It outlines the progression of researching an idea, reaching a target market and retaining a customer base. It is your own guide to what you hope to accomplish and of how you hope to accomplish it.

We hope that this book has given you some practical information and has helped you get your idea "Out of Your Mind...and Into the Marketplace™!"

Resources for Small Business

The Small Business Administration

The U.S. Small Business Administration is an independent federal agency that was created by Congress in 1953 to assist, counsel and represent small business. Statistics show that most small business failures are due to poor management. For this reason, the SBA places special emphasis on individual counseling, courses, conferences, workshops and publications to train the new and existing business owner in all facets of business development, with special emphasis on improving the management ability of the owner.

Counseling is provided through the Service Corps of Retired Executives (SCORE), Small Business Institutes (SBIs), Small Business Development Centers (SBDCs), and numerous professional associations. The SBA strives to match the need of a specific business with the expertise available.

Business management training covers such topics as planning, finance, organization and marketing and is held in cooperation with educational institutions, chambers of commerce and trade associations. Pre-business workshops are held on a regular basis for prospective business owners. Other training programs are conducted that focus on special needs such as rural development, young entrepreneurship and international trade. The following is a brief summary of what these programs include.

SCORE is a 13,000-person volunteer program with over 750 locations. SCORE helps small businesses solve their operating problems through one-on-one counseling and through a well developed system of workshops and training sessions. SCORE counseling is available at no charge.

Small Business Institutes (SBIs) are organized through the SBA on over 500 university and college campuses. At each SBI, on-site management counseling is provided by senior and graduate students at schools of business administration working with faculty advisors. In addition to counseling individual businesses, schools provide economic development assistance to communities. Students are guided by faculty advisors and SBA development staff and receive academic credit for their work.

Small Business Development Centers (SBDCs) draw their resources from local, state and federal government programs, the private sector and university facilities. They provide managerial and technical help, research studies and other types of specialized assistance. These centers are generally located or headquartered in academic institutions and provide individual counseling and practical training for small business owners.

Publications: Business Development has over 100 business publications which are available for a nominal fee. They address the most important questions asked by prospective and existing business owners. A free copy of *Directory of Business Development Publications* can be obtained by contacting your local SBA office or by calling the Small Business Answer Desk at (800) 827-5722 or by writing to: SBA, P.O. Box 46521, Denver, CO 80201.

Other Federal Resources

Many publications on business management and other related topics are available from the Government Printing Office (GPO). GPO bookstores are located in 24 major cities and are listed in the yellow pages under the "bookstore" heading. You can request a "Subject Bibliography" by writing to: Government Printing Office, Superintendent of Documents, Washington, DC 20402-9371.

Many federal agencies offer publications of interest to small businesses. There is a nominal fee for some, but most are free. Below is a partial list of government agencies that provide publications and other services targeted to small businesses. To get their publications, contact the regional offices listed in the telephone directory or write to the addresses below:

Bureau of the Census
Public Information Office
U.S. Department of Commerce
Washington, DC 20233
(301) 763-4051

Consumer Information Center (CIC)
P.O. Box 100
Pueblo, CO 81002

The CIC offers a consumer information catalog of federal publications.

Consumer Product Safety Commission (CPSC)
Publications Request
Washington, DC 20207

The CPSC offers guidelines for product safety requirements.

Data User Services Division
Customer Services
Bureau of the Census
Washington, DC 20233
(301) 763-4431

Federal Trade Commission
Office of Small and Disadvantaged Business Utilization
6th Street & Pennsylvania Avenue NW, Suite 700
Washington, DC 20580

U.S. Department of Agriculture (USDA)
12th Street and Independence Avenue, SW
Washington, DC 20250

Publications and programs on entrepreneurship are available through county extension offices nationwide.

U.S. Department of Commerce (DOC)
Office of Business Liaison
14th Street and Constitution Avenue, NW
Room 5898C
Washington, DC 20230

The DOC provides listings of business opportunities available in the federal government.

U.S. Department of Labor (DOL)
Employment Standards Administration
200 Constitution Avenue, NW
Washington, DC 20210

The DOL offers publications on compliance with labor laws.

U.S. Department of Treasury
Internal Revenue Service (IRS)
P.O. Box 25866
Richmond, VA 23260
(800) 424-3676

The IRS offers information on tax requirements for small businesses.

U.S. Environmental Protection Agency (EPA)
Small Business Ombudsman
401 M Street, SW (A-149C)
Washington, DC 20460

The EPA offers more than 100 publications designed to help small businesses understand how they can comply with EPA regulations.

U.S. Food and Drug Administration (FDA)
FDA Center for Food Safety and Applied Nutrition
200 Charles Street, SW
Washington, DC 20402

The FDA offers information on packaging and labeling requirements for food and food-related products.

Associations

American Management Association
135 West 50th Street
New York, NY 10020

Offers management assistance, including home-study courses on audio-cassette.

American Marketing Association
250 Wacker Drive, Suite 200
Chicago, IL 60606

Publishes annotated bibliographies on important marketing topics, conducts seminars and other educational programs.

Association of Collegiate Entrepreneurs (ACE)
Center for Entrepreneurship,
Box 147
Wichita State University,
Wichita, KS 67208

ACE members are student entrepreneurs. The organization holds regional and national conferences and acts as an information clearing house for young business founders.

International Council for Small Business
U.S. Association for Small Business and Entrepreneurs
905 University Avenue, Room 203
Madison, WI 53715

Professional organization for educators and entrepreneurs interested in the development of small business.

National Foundation for Women Business Owners (NFWBO)
1010 Wayne Avenue
Silver Springs, MD 20910

NFWBO is the National Association of Women Business Owners' non-profit research, leadership development, and entrepreneurial training foundation. Its mission is to support the growth of women business owners and their organizations through gathering and sharing knowledge.

National Federation of Independent Business
600 Maryland Avenue SW, Suite 700
Washington, DC 20024

The country's largest small business association, with more than 500,000 member business owners. In addition to representing small business interests to state and federal governments, it distributes educational information and publications, and holds conferences.

Library Resources

Bacon's Newspaper/Magazine Directory: Lists media as source of publicity information.

City and County Data Book: This book is updated every three years and contains statistical information on population, education, employment, income, housing and retail sales.

Dun and Bradstreet Directories: Lists companies alphabetically, geographically, and by product classification.

Encyclopedia of Associations: Lists trade and professional associations throughout the United States. Many publish newsletters and provide marketing information. These associations can help business owners keep up with the latest industry developments.

Encyclopedia of Business Information Sources: Lists handbooks, periodicals, directories, trade associations and more for over 1200 specific industries and business subjects. Start here to search information on your particular business.

Incubators for Small Business: Lists over 170 state government offices and incubators that offer financial and technical aid to new small businesses.

National Trade and Professional Associations of the U.S.: Trade and professional associations are indexed by association, geographic region, subject and budget.

Reference Book for World Traders: This three volume set lists banks, chambers of commerce, customs, marketing organizations, invoicing procedures, and more for 185 foreign markets. Sections on export planning, financing, shipping, laws and tariffs are also included, with a directory of helpful government agencies.

Small Business Sourcebook: A good starting place for finding consultants, educational institutions, and governmental agencies offering assistance, as well as specific information sources for over 140 types of businesses.

Sourcebook for Franchise Opportunities: Provides annual directory information for U.S. franchises and data for investment requirements, royalty and advertising fees, services furnished by the franchiser, projected growth rates and locations where franchises are licensed to operate.

World Trade Outlook: Examines trends and provides forecasts for industries in terms of international trade.

Worksheets

The blank forms and worksheets are for you to fill out and use.

Questionnaire Coding Log

Code	Date	No. Sent	Destination/Recipient	Response Rate	Evaluation

Market Research Worksheet

Questions	Information Source	Results	Effect on Plan

Target Market Worksheet

1. WHO ARE MY CUSTOMERS?

Profile:

Economic level:

Psychological make-up (lifestyle):

Age range:

Sex:

Income level:

Buying habits:

2. WHERE ARE MY CUSTOMERS LOCATED?

Where do they live:

Where do they work:

Where do they shop:

3. PROJECTED SIZE OF THE MARKET:

4. WHAT ARE THE CUSTOMERS NEEDS?

a.

b.

c.

d.

e.

f.

5. HOW CAN I MEET THOSE NEEDS?

a.

b.

c.

d.

e.

f.

6. WHAT IS UNIQUE ABOUT MY BUSINESS?

Location Analysis Worksheet

1. ADDRESS:

2. NAME, ADDRESS, PHONE NUMBER OF REALTOR/CONTACT PERSON:

3. SQUARE FOOTAGE/COST:

4. HISTORY OF LOCATION:

5. LOCATION IN RELATION TO TARGET MARKET:

6. TRAFFIC PATTERNS FOR CUSTOMERS:

7. TRAFFIC PATTERNS FOR SUPPLIERS:

8. AVAILABILITY OF PARKING (include diagram):

9. CRIME RATE FOR THE AREA:

10. QUALITY OF PUBLIC SERVICES (e.g., police, fire protection):

11. NOTES OF WALKING TOUR OF THE AREA:

12. NEIGHBORING SHOPS AND LOCAL BUSINESS CLIMATE:

13. ZONING REGULATIONS:

14. ADEQUACY OF UTILITIES (get information from utility company representatives):

15. AVAILABILITY OF RAW MATERIALS/SUPPLIES:

16. AVAILABILITY OF LABOR FORCE:

17. LABOR RATE OF PAY FOR THE AREA:

18. HOUSING AVAILABILITY FOR EMPLOYEES:

19. TAX RATES (state, county, income, payroll, special assessments):

20. EVALUATION OF SITE IN RELATION TO COMPETITION:

Competition Evaluation Form

PROFILE OF THE COMPETITION

1. COMPETITOR:

2. LOCATION:

3. PRODUCTS OR SERVICES OFFERED:

4. METHODS OF DISTRIBUTION:

5. IMAGE:

   Packaging:

   Promotional materials:

   Methods of advertising:

   Quality of product or service:

6. PRICING STRUCTURE:

7. BUSINESS HISTORY & CURRENT PERFORMANCE:

8. MARKET SHARE (number, types and location of customers):

9. STRENGTHS (the strengths of the competition become your strengths):

10. WEAKNESSES (looking at the weaknesses of the competition can help you find ways of being unique and of benefiting the customer):

Cash to be Paid Out Worksheet
(Cash Flowing Out of the Business)

Time Period Covered: _____ ___, 19___ to _____ ___, 19___

1. START-UP COSTS $ _____
     Business License   _____
     Corporation Filing   _____
     Legal Fees   _____
     Other startup costs:
        a.   _____
        b.   _____
        c.   _____

2. INVENTORY PURCHASES
     Cash out for goods intended for resale   _____

3. VARIABLE EXPENSES (SELLING)
        a.   _____
        b.   _____
        c.   _____
        d.   _____
        e.   _____
        f.   _____
        g. Miscellaneous Selling Expense   _____
TOTAL SELLING EXPENSES   _____

4. FIXED EXPENSES (ADMIN)
        a.   _____
        b.   _____
        c.   _____
        d.   _____
        e.   _____
        f.   _____
        g. Miscellaneous Administrative Expense   _____
TOTAL ADMINISTRATIVE EXPENSE   _____

5. ASSETS (LONG-TERM PURCHASES)   _____
     Cash to be paid out in current period

6. LIABILITIES
     Cash outlay for retiring debts, loans   _____
     and/or accounts payable

7. OWNER EQUITY
     Cash to be withdrawn by owner   _____

TOTAL CASH TO BE PAID OUT $ _____

Advertising Worksheet

Name of business:

1. What are the features and benefits of my product or service?

2. Who is my audience?

3. Who is my competition and how do they advertise?

4. What are the goals of my advertising campaign?

5. How much do I plan to invest for advertising?

6. What advertising methods will I use?

__ Newspapers	__ Magazines	__ Yellow pages
__ Radio	__ Television	__ Direct mail
__ Telemarketing	__ Flyers	__ Brochures
__ Coupons	__ Press release	__ Promo items

__ Other _____

7. When will I use them and what will they cost?

8. How will I measure the effectiveness of the advertising plan?

Advertising Response Record

Company Name: _____

Type of Ad	Date Run	Cost	Circulation	No. Responses	Income Generated

Publicity Tracking Record

Company Name: _____

Media Name	Contact Person	Address	Date	Material Sent	Follow-Up	Response	Results	Notes

Glossary of Marketing Terms

Advertising: The practice of bringing to the public's notice the good qualities of something in order to induce the public to buy or invest in it.

Benchmarking: Rating your company's products, services and practices against those of the front-runners in the industry.

Bill of lading: A document issued by a railroad or other carrier. It acknowledges the receipt of specified goods for transportation to a certain place, it sets forth the contract between the shipper and the carrier, and it provides for proper delivery of the goods.

Bill of sale: A formal legal document that conveys title to or right of interest in specific personal property from the seller to the buyer.

Brand name: A term, symbol, design or combination thereof that identifies and differentiates a seller's products or service.

Chamber of Commerce: An organization of business people designed to advance the interests of its members. There are three levels: national, state and local.

Choice: A decision to purchase that is based on an evaluation of alternatives.

Commission: A percentage of the principal or of the income that an agent receives as compensation for services.

Cost of good sold: The direct cost to the business owner of those items that will be sold to customers. The cost of raw materials plus the cost of labor in the production of a product.

Differentiated marketing: Selecting and developing a number of offerings to meet the needs of a number of specific market segments.

Direct mail: Marketing goods or services directly to the consumer through the mail.

Direct selling: The process whereby the producer sells to the user, ultimate consumer or retailer without intervening middlemen.

Discount: A deduction from the stated or list price of a product or service.

Distribution channel: All of the individuals and organizations involved in the process of moving products from producer to consumer. The route a product follows as it moves from the original grower, producer or importer to the ultimate consumer.

Entrepreneur: An innovator of business enterprise who recognizes opportunities to introduce a new product, a new process or an improved organization, and who raises the necessary money, assembles the factors for production and organizes an operation to exploit the opportunity.

Exchange: The process by which two or more parties give something of value to one another to satisfy needs and wants.

Gross profit: The difference between the selling price and the cost of an item. Gross profit is calculated by subtracting the cost of goods sold from net sales.

Inventory: A list of assets being held for sale.

Keystone: Setting a retail price at twice the wholesale price.

Lead: The name and address of a possible customer.

Life-style: A pattern of living that comprises an individual's activities, interests, and opinions.

Market: A set of potential or real buyers, or a place in which there is a demand for products or services. Actual or potential buyers of a product or service.

Market demand: Total volume purchased in a specific geographic area by a specific customer group in a specified time period under a specified marketing program.

Market forecast: An anticipated demand that results from a planned marketing expenditure.

Market share: A company's percentage share of total sales within a given market.

Marketing mix: The set of product, place, promotion, price and packaging variables that a marketing manager controls and orchestrates to bring a product or service into the marketplace.

Market positioning: Finding a market niche that emphasizes the strengths of a product or service in relation to the weaknesses of the competition.

Marketing research: The systematic design, collection, analysis and reporting of data regarding a specific marketing situation.

Market targeting: Choosing a marketing strategy in terms of competitive strengths and marketplace realities.

Mass marketing: Selecting and developing a single offering for an entire market.

Middleman: A person or company who performs functions or renders services involved in the purchase and/or sale of goods in their flow from producer to consumer.

Need: A state of perceived deprivation.

Niche: A well-defined group of customers for which the product or service you have to offer is particularly suitable.

Organizational market: A marketplace made up of producers, trade industries, governments and institutions.

Overhead: A general term for costs of materials and services not directly adding to or readily identifiable with the product or service being sold.

Perception: The process of selecting, organizing and interpreting information received through the senses.

Price: The exchange value of a product or service from the perspective of both the buyer and the seller.

Price ceiling: The highest amount that a customer will pay for a product or a service based upon perceived value.

Price floor: The lowest amount a business owner can charge for a product or service and still meet all expenses.

Price planning: The systematic process for establishing pricing objectives and policies.

Producers: The components of the organizational market that acquire products and services that enter into the production of products and services that are sold or supplied to others.

Product life cycle: The stages of development and decline through which a successful product typically moves. Often referred to as "PLC."

Product line: A group of products related to each other by marketing, technical or end-use considerations.

Product mix: All of the products in a seller's total product line.

Products: Anything capable of satisfying needs, including tangible items, services, and ideas.

Profit: Financial gain, returns over expenditures.

Profit margin: The difference between your selling price and all of your costs.

Promotion: The communication of information by a seller to influence the attitudes and behavior of potential buyers.

Promotional pricing: Temporarily pricing a product or service below list price or below cost in order to attract customers.

Psychographics: The system of explaining market behavior in terms of attitudes and life-styles.

Publicity: Any non-paid, news-oriented presentation of a product, service or business entity in a mass media format.

Quantitative forecasts: Forecasts that are based on measurements of numerical quantities.

Questionnaire: A data-gathering form used to collect information by a personal interview, with a telephone survey or through the mail.

Retailing: Businesses and individuals engaged in the activity of selling products to final consumers.

Revenue: Total sales during a stated period.

Sales potential: A company's expected share of a market as marketing expenditures increase in relation to the competition.

Sales promotion: Marketing activities that stimulate consumer purchasing in the short term.

Sales representative: An independent salesperson who directs efforts to selling your products or service to others but is not an employee of your company. Sales reps often represent more than one product line from more than one company and usually work on commission.

Sample: A limited portion of the whole of a group.

Service business: A business that does things for you, rather than sells you goods. Examples include utilities providing telephone and transportation service as well as trades and professions such as laundry, repair, consulting, and maintenance help.

Suppliers: Individuals or businesses that provide resources needed by a company and its competitors in order to produce goods and services.

Survey: A research method in which people are asked questions.

Target market: The specific individuals, distinguished by socio-economic, demographic and interest characteristics, who are the most likely potential customers for the goods and services of a business.

Target marketing: Selecting and developing a number of offerings to meet the needs of a number of specific market segments.

Undifferentiated marketing: Selecting and developing one offering for an entire market.

Wholesale: Selling for resale.

Wholesaling: Businesses and individuals engaged in the activity of selling products to retailers, organizational users or other wholesalers.

Index

A

Active business activity, 9

Address code, 29

Advertising, 96-99, 106, 111, 113-114

Age distribution, trends in, 52

American Management Association, 144

American Marketing Association, 6, 144

Association of Collegiate Entrepreneurs (ACE), 145

Associations, 144-145

B

Billable hours, 87-88

Books, publications and references: communications, 137-138; competition evaluation, 47-48; on packaging, 119-120; patent and copyright, 16-17; on place, 80; on pricing, 90; product and service, 67-68; promotion, 104-105; on questionnaires, 30; on surveying the market, 6; target market, 56-57; on test marketing, 40

Brochures, advertising, 101, 110

Bureau of Consumer Protection, 40, 121

Business cards, 117-118

Business incubators, 79

Buying habits/trends, 3-4

Buying style, market, 54

C

Cash paid out, example worksheet, 92-93

Catalogs, 72-73

Colors, company, 116

Communication: community involvement, 136; customer feedback, 134-135; with employees, 135-136; mailing lists, 133-134

Community involvement: advertising and, 100; communication and, 136

Competition: evaluating the, 43-49; location of, 78

Complaints: employee oriented, 126-127; establishing a complaint system, 134-135; location oriented, 127; product or service oriented, 128

Consignments, 73-74

Consumer Products Safety Commission, 40, 68, 121

Copyright, 10-12, 16-17

Copyright Office, 16

Cost: business location, 78; co-op cost sharing, 101

Cost of goods to be sold (inventory), 86-87

Council of Logistics Management, 80

Customer feedback, 134-135

Customer satisfaction, 129-131

Customer service, 125-128

Customer, uniqueness and benefits to the: advertising, 96; competition evaluation, 45

D

Demographics, 51-53

Depository Libraries, 14

Desired annual net income, 87

Direct competition, 43

Direct mail: advertising, 101; questionnaires, 27-28

Direct Mail/Marketing Association, 30, 105

Direct sales, 72

Disclosure document, patent, 14

Disclosure letter, 9

Discounts, offering, 102

Displays, marketing, 100

Distribution, methods of, 71-76

Drop shipments, 73

E

Education level, occupation, and income, 53

Employees: availability of, 78; communicating with, 135-136; employee oriented complaints, 126-127

Endorsements and testimonials, 39

Enterprise zones, 79

Ethnic origin, population based on, 52

F

Fads, 3-4